Midwest Gardens

Midwest Gardens

Pamela Wolfe

——

Photographs by Gary Irving

Chicago Review Press

Library of Congress Cataloging-in-Publication Data
Wolfe, Pamela.
    Midwest gardens / Pam Wolfe; photographs by Gary Irving.
    p. cm.
    Includes bibliographical references and index.
    Hardcover ISBN 1-55652-138-3 : $39.95 Paperback ISBN 1-55652-309-2:
    $29.95
    1. Landscape gardening — Middle West. 2. Gardens — Middle West
3. Gardens — Middle West — Pictorial works. I. Irving, Gary.
II. Title.
SB473.W57 1991
635'.0977 — dc20   91-25570
                                                                  CIP

Published by Chicago Review Press, Incorporated
814 North Franklin Street
Chicago, Illinois 60610
ISBN 1-55652-309-2
Printed in Hong Kong by Lammar Printing

1 2 3 4 5

For my mother,
Ruby Davidson Cornell,
the first and foremost gardener in my life.

Contents

Photographer's Preface

In May 1989, when Pam Wolfe first approached me with her idea of collaborating on a book of midwestern gardens, I was preparing to leave a state position as photographer at the Morton Arboretum in Lisle, Illinois, to devote my time to more personal photographic pursuits, including a book of panoramic views of rural Illinois. Thus, I was in the middle of a project that allowed me to explore the exhilarating dimensions of the long horizontal line and observe the play of light on the midwestern landscape. So when Pam began to describe her idea to photographically depict an eclectic garden tour in the Midwest, I was intrigued.

My approach in this book is quite different from the previous landscape volume. I found early on that I was not working with space and light but rather in terms of color, texture, and pattern. Instead of panoramic overviews, I found myself working in tight, intimate spaces, trying to see the garden as the gardener does, down on bended knee. While Pam is an expert gardener, my own property bears witness that I am not. However, it was possible that I might bring a fresh, unbiased eye to each of these lovely gardens in a way that might complement her more informed observations. I hope you will find this to be the case.

It was a pleasure and a challenge to walk these gardens, trying to reveal each garden's personality without losing my own sense of place. The logistics of trying to be present at peak periods of color in twenty-two gardens in an area as large as the Upper Midwest are difficult at best. We visited some gardens once or twice, some many times. We have tried to provide enough of an honest sampling to allow your imagination to begin to think of possibilities, however modest, for your own Midwest Garden.

Gary Irving

Acknowledgments

The encouragement and direction I have tried to pass on to Midwest gardeners in this book was granted to me in the truest fashion. As a teacher and horticulturist this project came as naturally as breathing, but my attempts would have been feeble without help from so many.

The direct inspiration for this book came from a student of mine at the Morton Arboretum in Lisle, Illinois. She asked simply, "What's a good book I can get on perennial gardens in the Midwest? All the books seem to be written for English or eastern gardens. I want examples of gardens in this area." I didn't have an immediate answer. But the idea was "planted!" Since Gary Irving, a noted photographer and a colleague at the arboretum, was finishing a project, I suggested that next he photograph midwestern gardens. He agreed.

I want to thank my friend and colleague, Elsie Stiffler, for her steadfast encouragement and guidance. Her support, confidence, and expertise gave form to my ideas. She listened and advised yet always let me speak with my own voice—the hallmark of an outstanding teacher.

My sincere appreciation to my editor, Amy Teschner, whose talent and patience refined my work with considerable success. I want to recognize Fran Lee for the elegant job she did designing the book, and I value the expert technical editing by Gilbert S. Daniels. My genuine thanks to Jane Rundell, Laura Larson, and Eunice Hoshizaki for riding shotgun on the road toward literary correctness, and to Bebe Mosillo for all the support on the path toward computer literacy.

Others I want to thank from the Morton Arboretum—for supporting my efforts and helping me find outstanding gardens—include Ross Clark, Ian McPhail, Peter van der Linden, Bill Hess,

Tony Tyznik, Charles Lewis, Floyd Swink, Mary Hason, and Linda Sanford.

I want to recognize Jim Schuster, Extension Advisor for the University of Illinois Cooperative Extension Service in DuPage County, for his help in answering my technical questions, not just now, but over the last twenty years. I also appreciate meeting many outstanding Master Gardeners. The Cooperative Extension Agents Mike Dana from Purdue University; Mark Kepler from Lake County, Indiana; Allen Boger from Allen County, Indiana; Marcia Pyicka from Will County, Illinois, Helen Harrison, from the University of Wisconsin; and the Master Gardeners Mary Tennent, Warren Seinnke, Mary Gall, and Barb Kirby were very helpful.

Others who graciously aided me were Dan Cooper from the Iowa Department of Agriculture and Land Stewardship; Dianne Noland from the University of Illinois; Nancy Allison from the Minnesota Landscape Arboretum; Gene Heinemann from the Dubuque Arboretum and Botanical Gardens; Deon Prell, a garden designer from Troy, Wisconsin; Evelyn Clemmens, a landscape designer from Glenn Ellyn, Illinois; Vicki Behm from Rosenzweig Design in Chicago; Mark Zilis of Planter's Palette in Winfield, Illinois; and Dan Beikmann from Fernwood Nature Center in Niles, Michigan.

Garden club members from several states assisted me, including Rosemary Hatfield, Jan St. John, Rita Wisniewski, Marilyn Ellison, Betty Collings, Meg Starr, La Vern Laycock, Iemundine Breymann, and Susan Beard. And special appreciation goes to Lori Otto, Lucy Schumann, and the garden organization The Wild Ones, for sharing with me the important work they are doing in saving native plants and starting native gardens. Thanks so much to friends and colleagues Susan Cantrell, Betty White, Ted Teal, Bill Hills, Mike and Diana Scheer, Suzanne Millies, Marie Starsiak, Frew Brown, Larry Langellier, and Mary Ann Janiak.

Over the past three years many people helped in my search for exceptional Midwest gardens. We were limited by time and space and could not include all that I learned about, because the Midwest has an abundance of talented, innovative gardeners.

I want to express my appreciation to all the gardeners in this book. One satisfying outcome of the book's research is the feeling that I have more than twenty-two new gardening friends. I gained much from visiting these and other gardens over the last three years.

A personal note of thanks to my father, who showed me it is possible to work twenty-two hours a day, and to my loving husband, Bruce, who patiently supported me while I did it. And warm, teary gratitude to my daughters, Andrea and Meredith—who cooked, gardened, did the laundry, and helped their dad take up the slack. This is their effort as well. I cannot say enough about the backing of my dear family, what it means to me, and to what relief they see this book finished.

When I think of the next generation of gardeners, my mind drifts back. I want to thank the grandmother I never met for wonderful, enchanting memories: as a very young child I loved to sit in a small sumac tree near her rock garden. The garden was built with stones carried from nearby Sugar Creek and pocketed with water worn holes which held the little sempervivums. Her goldfish pond was made from collected rocks cemented together. Nearby stood the row of hollyhocks. Most of all I remember the cotillion of hollyhock dolls who danced for hours on the back porch in the summer. Gardens are for dreams and for dreamers.

Pamela Wolfe

Introduction

The Midwest? Peel off the two coasts and their mountains. Take off the Southwest, the South, and Texas. What is left we call the "Midwest." All the people I met as a college student in Ohio, from anywhere east of that state considered themselves "Out West." And those who lived a couple states west of Ohio felt that they had come "East" to school. I concluded early on that the Midwest, like its modern synonym, the "Heartland," is somewhat a matter of perspective. Anyone who has lived here in the "Provinces" knows that the region does not stand up to the short, monolithic labels usually afforded it, but we're rather quiet about it.

Very few of the many excellent garden books give in-depth information specifically for the midwestern garden. Most garden literature focuses on coastal or English gardens, and many of these fine references state that the gardener may have to "adjust" the information for his or her own location. Since "adjusting" really means the information will not work everywhere, midwestern gardeners are still on their own to experiment and find out what really grows.

In the twenty-two gardens highlighted on these pages, the Midwest's rich diversity comes alive. While visiting gardens for this book, I traveled fourteen thousand miles and never did get to North and South Dakota, Nebraska, Kansas, or Missouri, or for that matter the state of my alma mater, Ohio. The area I was led to call the Midwest includes Minnesota, Wisconsin, Michigan, Indiana, Illinois, and Iowa—a sizable chunk, to be sure. And here I found an incredible variety of gardening styles and environments.

Every gardener has to contend with soil first. True to its image, the Midwest I visited supplies plenty of deep, rich topsoil. But simply referring to "rich topsoil" does not really give a gardener much useful information. I suspect that many new gardeners do not know what topsoil means, except that it is on top! The most general difference between the soils I saw on my midwestern travels and that of other parts of the country is that the Midwest is short on "red dirt" and few of its gardeners grow ericaceous plants.

The general soil characteristic comes from the limestone base of much of the area and the glacial origin of the soil. This gives the soil a predominately mineral nature with a neutral or slightly higher pH. The exceptions are pockets of the highly organic "muck" soils, which grow acid-loving plants more easily.

One little-acknowledged aspect of midwestern soil was taught to most of us as young students. We learned that the prairies were not widely farmed until Cyrus McCormick developed the steel plow. The inference seems obvious, yet it's ignored: the Midwest has very difficult soils to dig. The fact that these heavy, rich soils grow weeds better than anywhere else in the country—perhaps the world—is further ignored! Weeds grow deeper, bigger, and faster in the Midwest than most of us want to admit. When my daughter was born in May one year, my gardening was severely curtailed for a season. I can still see, in my mind's eye, one particular weed towering in the garden. I stood bleary-eyed, looking at it from my kitchen window and thinking, "I didn't know that one grew that tall!"

Sadly, in my teaching experience I have seen weeds "do in" the most enthusiastic gardener. We are in a part of the country where if you mow an area often enough, you will get a lawn. It may not be uniform, but it will be green and three inches tall. Never minimize the effect of weeds on the spirit of the gardener, but realize many gardeners have overcome this obstacle through patience and ingenuity.

As if the soil is not enough to contend with, the climate in the Midwest is not a drawing card for many people. When I was a young Hoosier, I had an uncle who used to visit us from California every six or so years. He and my aunt brought their family East in the summer for this reunion. During these visits I remember seeing my cousin suffer from hay fever, and my uncle asked me how I could stand to live in an area with such heat and humidity. (All the corn on the cob and homemade ice cream didn't seem to help.) I remember answering that it wasn't like this all year long! He looked indulgently at me and smiled.

For a gardener, the midwestern climate poses many significant barriers. The intense summer heat kills many plants that thrive in more consistently cool regions. This heat is accompanied by the characteristically low rainfall of a grassland, which often comes as an intermittent drought rather than a low, steady amount of water. So when the heat and drought don't kill them, many perennials die from drowning. And if this isn't stress enough, the humidity that blankets the summer encourages a variety of problems, including mildew, botrytis (gray mold), and leaf-spot diseases.

But the real killer remains cold weather. As most gardeners know, the average minimum temperature dictates which plants will grow in a region, and those temperature zones are listed in most catalogs. Since the Midwest's cold winters make it predominately zones 4 and 5, the selection of plants is somewhat limited. However, the zone designation disregards the subtle problems of cold weather. Very rapid cooling in the autumn that freezes the ground in a matter of days rather than weeks kills roses. January thaws, followed by frigid February storms, can take their toll on everything. In late winter, as the ground is warming, a sudden cold snap may rip at the roots that survived the coldest days of winter. Shallow-rooted plants suffer the most. The action of freezing and thawing breaks up the garden just as it does the concrete and asphalt streets. The subsequent spring rains wash away all the fissures—not to be noticed, except for the dead plants.

Yet many plants do survive, even thrive, in this environment. In the right spot indigenous plants will grow. But since ancient times, travelers have imported plants from one area to another looking for new and "better" plants. Many survive and indeed spread rapidly in their new environment; some beautiful ones even thrive, but they do so too easily. Presently, our native wetland areas are particularly threatened by a lovely, tall plant called purple loosestrife *(Lythrum salicaria)*. It spreads rapidly by seeds through wetland areas, choking out native species and decreasing natural variety. In an effort to protect native habitats, many midwestern states prohibit sales of the plant. Cultivars exist, like *Lythrum* 'Morden Pink' and 'Morden Gleam', that are less likely to self-seed, yet accurate identification of the plants makes even the sale of these restricted.

In this book I show success stories and introduce you to people who live with the soil and the climate and who make it work for them. Discovering different techniques for handling soil and observing what gardeners grow in the different soil types made all the hours of traveling worthwhile for me, and I am excited to share what I learned with other gardeners. I found gardeners enjoying their hot, muggy summers and cold, fluctuating winters. I found them working with their environment, catching rainwater, making compost, and using predators like ladybug beetles. I found them arranging their gardens like bouquets, blending and mixing the most interesting combinations. I found them enjoying their gardens.

The variety of gardens in the Midwest will surprise many, especially those who have yet to garden in the region. The ranges of climate and soil make it difficult to sum up in a very few words what the Midwest is like. That seems fitting when you consider the many gardening designs found here. The variety of styles in these twenty-two gardens will give fresh ideas to even the most experienced gardener.

I hope for *Midwest Gardens* to be an inspiration as well as a practical guide. With these good gardening examples, I want to encourage more gardeners, more stewards of the land. Through the ingenuity of these twenty-two gardeners and Gary Irving's creative eye, the vast area known as the Midwest is more completely defined.

It is not simply potatoes and beets
*   and corn and cucumbers*
that one raises in his well-hoed garden;
it is the average of human life.

There is life in the ground,
it goes into the seeds
and it also, when it is stirred up,
goes into the man who stirs it.

The hot sun on his back as he bends
*   to his shovel or hoe,*
*   or contemplatively rakes*
*   the warm and fragrant loam*
is better than much medicine. . . .

To own a bit of ground,
*   to scratch it with a hoe*
*   to plant seeds and*
*   to watch the renewal of life,*
this is the commonest delight of the race,
the most satisfactory thing a man can do.

Charles Dudley Warner
1829–1900

Monee, Illinois
THE SHAW FAMILY

The Shaw family gardens, located on two adjoining pieces of land in central Illinois, are beautifully crowded. The asters get so tall that they gently flop over nearby plants like the downy phlox *(Phlox pilosa)*. And sturdy prairie plants like cordgrass, *(Spartina pectinata)* and the sunflower *(Helianthus* sp.) seem determined to push out the big blue stem *(Andropogon gerardii)*, although fortunately they have not yet succeeded.

The juxtaposition of so many flourishing plants, nonnative varieties thriving beside native ones, has been achieved by four different gardeners working together.

Each of the gardening Shaws—Connor III; his wife, Joanne; his father, Connor II; and his mother, Betty—has a unique style that combines splendidly with those

Single flowering garden peony.

of the other three. Connor III owns and operates Possibility Place Nursery, which specializes in native, woody plants. In his gardens Connor III uses all plants indigenous to the area. He blends groups of native trees and shrubs with native herbaceous plants, building gardens that are uniquely midwestern. Joanne is groundskeeper at Governor's State University in University Park, Illinois. At home she cultivates an herb and cutting garden a few steps from her kitchen door.

Connor II and Betty live next door and maintain an extensive garden developed over twenty years. Connor II begins with a backbone of native plants, but adds an entire array of plants useful for the garden, while Betty's interest in the rose garden stimulates creative grow-

Left: In container, Lantana; marigolds in foreground, phlox *(Phlox paniculata* 'Mt. Fujiyama'); in background, island bed with white flowering tobacco *(Nicotiana alata).*

ing techniques. By using native prairie plants in an ornamental rather than natural design, Connor III emphasizes the gardener's role and makes the Shaw family gardens a tribute not only to nature but to the gardener's creativity.

Masses of prairie grasses like prairie dropseed (*Sporobolus heterolepis*) are set next to clumps of purple coneflower (*Echinacea purpurea*) and rattlesnake master (*Eryngium yuccifolium*) in a flowing pattern resembling an English cottage garden or the New American gardens of Jim van Sweden and Wolfgang Oehme. Instead of crocus and tulips, patches of shooting star (*Dodecatheon meadia*) and pasque flowers (*Anemone patens*), native to the midwestern prairie, greet the first days of spring.

More than thirty-five species of native prairie plants give a showy display of plants fully adapted to the extremes of this climate. This walkway garden has been developed piece by piece over a period of four years, resulting in plants and plant combinations that bloom successively. Plants like *Liatris, Rudbeckia, Coreopsis, Physostegia*, and *Echinacea* plus other sturdy natives produce a spectacular effect. Prairie dock (*Silphium terebinthinaceum*), compass plant (*Silphium laciniatum*), and stiff coreopsis (*Coreopsis palmata*) produce an attractive, grassy stand with flecks of color. The smaller and more delicate prairie

smoke (*Geum triflorum*) blooms and expands easily without being invasive. Says the younger Connor, "Prairie smoke is a phenomenal ground cover. It's very attractive in all seasons in full sun or light shade, and it's semievergreen."

In both gardens a wide variety of tall and medium shrubs fills out the

Purple coneflower (*Echinacea purpurea*); globe thistle (*Echinops ritro*).

landscape with a luxuriant combination of woody and herbaceous plants. *Ribes alpinum* serves as a backdrop for Connor II's daylilies in a corner planting of the house. The catkins of the tall *Corylus americana* hang like ornaments at one end of a long sweeping

display. Shrub roses and native viburnums give the beds depth and texture in all seasons, and the small native fringe tree adds a wonderful fragrance. He emphasizes, "Mixing shrubs with perennials gives it some winter effect too or fills in when a short-lived perennial dies and leaves a hole."

Connor III arranges his trees and shrubs differently than he treats the native prairie plants, using an informal, natural flow. In order to produce a natural-looking garden and landscape, he suggests using plants of an uneven age and size to give the garden a sense of progression. "It is common practice to bring in fifty shrubs that are all five feet tall and arrange them in a line that's perfectly straight head-on instead of having a natural effect. My teacher was the woods and all that's native out there. When going down the Kankakee River, if you see one river birch you see several in a cluster. I've seen clusters of persimmon, and seen clusters of oak, and everyone wants to plant them on thirty-foot centers. They're in groupings in the landscapes, and that's the way we have to portray them. The only way to get birds in the yard is by cover, and you've got to put a lot of plant material down to get cover."

He advocates planting seven locally native species of oaks. The burr, chinquapin, white, Hill's oak, swamp white, shingle, and red oak are better suited to the soil and environmental stresses than many commonly used trees. He finds the durability of the native oaks impressive and combines them with native shrubs like the blackhaw viburnum (*Viburnum prunifolium*), spice bush (*Lindera benzoin*), and the yellow honeysuckle (*Lonicera prolifera*), which he chooses as attractive, disease-resistant alternatives to the more delicate Eurasian species.

Like herbaceous plants, trees and shrubs have growing requirements, so when Conner III places them in the garden he reads the landscape. In a climate where the soil drains slowly and the temperature shifts are dramatic, the "right" location requires more information than "sun" or "shade." Cornelian cherry dogwood (*Cornus mas*), a beautiful plant whose small yellow flowers light up the very early spring, dries out quickly. But *Potentilla fruticosa*, whose yellow flowers carry many gardens right through the hottest part of the summer, resists drying out. Connor III considers placement "very important." "For instance," he says, "if you put a redbud on a southwest corner of a house, it's going to die, even an old one. And pagoda dogwood has to be in shade; they can't take full sun. Oakleaf hydrangea can be planted near a downspout where runoff from the slightest rain will water it."

Although Connor III grows primarily native plants, Joanne uses nonnatives as well. Since she enjoys using herbs and flowers from her garden, she designed the bed at the kitchen door for color and for her use. She arranges patches of yarrow and chives mixed with lavender and baby's breath in eye-catching combi-

Shasta daisy (*Chrysanthemum x superbum*); garden pinks (*Dianthus alpinus* 'Alwoodii'); pink peony (*Paeonia lactiflora*); coreopsis budding (*Coreopsis verticillata* 'Zagreb').

nations, and plants in beds are raised above the surrounding landscape. Soil taken from the south side of their home and piled along the north creates a passive solar energy design as well as providing raised planting beds near the kitchen door, which drain

more efficiently than the surrounding heavy clay soil. Although the grade change helps these beds drain more efficiently, the Shaws amend the soils regularly since the soil piled to make the berm contains predominately subsoil rather than topsoil rich in organic matter. Connor III recalls, "We put four to six inches of topsoil, then six inches of manure, and rototilled it all together. Now we add compost to it every fall."

Standing tall, yarrow withstands strong winds and heavy rains in Jo's kitchen door garden. *Achillea filipendula* 'Cloth of Gold' with flat, bright yellow flower heads sitting over finely cut foliage on two-to-three-foot stems gives a colorful background to the garden and provides flowers for both summer and fall bouquets. Protected from the strongest gusts across the prairies by the house and the shorter plants in front, yarrow glows like a beacon in the summer sun. Flanking the yarrow are graceful masses of lovage, liatris, and sage. Lovage grows in lacy five-foot clumps and provides Jo's kitchen with an herb similar to celery. Although much shorter, sage's persistent gray-green two-foot mounds add interesting color and texture to the winter garden. And the plumes of liatris are excellent in fresh or dried bouquets. Nearby catmint (*Nepeta mussinii*), a delicate blue, and garlic chives (*Allium tuberosum*), spreading spheres of white, complement the yellow drifts of *Coreopsis verticillata* and clumps of coneflowers (*Rudbeckia fulgida* var. *sullivantii*). Jo picks the flowers of garlic chives to prevent sprouts throughout the garden. They make attractive fresh or dried-flower arrangements. Except for mountain mint (*Pycnanthemum muticum*), a strongly fragrant mint that keeps in bounds, mints, planted in clay pots and buried in the ground, add to the culinary and foliage display.

The three- to four-foot mass of the pink, single shrub rose, 'Bonica', fits into the predominately yellow and lavender display well and requires little maintenance. In early spring the shasta daisies turn the garden to a mass of white, followed by the Siberian iris with shades of blue, then the profusion of blue and pink larkspur, which seed at will and rise above the other emerging herbs and summer bloomers.

Receiving some attention to soil amendment, the fully hardy, if less colorful, *Heuchera richardsonii* produces wispy, light green flowers and coppery-colored foliage and grows more tenaciously, showing off the fall garden with tones of a woodland scene. Many native plants have excellent fall color and add depth to the garden by lengthening the season. Connor III states, "Everybody goes to the woods to see fall color because they don't have it in their yard."

Providing each bed with adequate water determines the success of the garden. When the rain gauge measures less than an inch of water per week, the Shaws consider it a signal to add water. The drip irrigation system begins to flow when the plants show signs of stress like wilting. In this way, plants get water only when

Phlox paniculata; white flowering tobacco (*Nicotiana alata*).

rainfall fails to provide adequate moisture. Connor II points out, "An inch of water per week is adequate under certain circumstances, but if it is ninety-five degrees and you've got a brisk wind and it stays ninety-five degrees for three or four days, plants

will have to have more water. When it's cool and cloudy and you get some rain, even though you might not get an inch, that can be adequate."

The Shaw gardens develop by trial and error. A large selection of plants grow in rich soil that is well drained, but shallow, fibrous-rooted plants like dianthus are not always dependable here. They often last one or two years and then die off. Some shallow-rooted heucheras tend to heave out of the ground in the late winter and early spring cycles of freezing and thawing, reducing their dependability. Wet springs and late freezes kill the largest number of perennials that manage to survive the cold temperatures, second only to the winter kill resulting from low temperatures with no snow cover or winter protective mulch. This freezing and thawing of exposed ground heaves plants out of the ground, killing them by ripping their roots.

To help roses survive the severe swings of winter, Connor II plants each bush with the graft union one foot below ground level. This unique technique breaks with the usual practice of planting the graft at or slightly above the surface of the soil. Besides this protection, each bush gets additional mounding with leaves and straw in late fall to reduce winter des-

Prairie coreopsis (*Coreopsis palmata*); black-eyed Susan (*Rudbeckia hirta*); rattlesnake master (*Eryngium yuccifolium*); false dragonhead (*Physostegia virginiana*).

iccation of the canes. The light, well-drained soil for this rose bed took several years to develop from the native soil. But now, rather than smothering in thick, heavy clay, the soil insulates the bushes and promotes new roots from the canes of the desired cultivar. Roses drown and rot in soil that does not drain rapidly, particularly as the soil freezes. For this reason growing roses in the Midwest takes the extra work of amending the soil and protecting the canes against the drying winter winds.

During the growing season, a layer of mulch around the plant helps reduce the temperature swings of summer as well. Connor II comments, "I mulch all the time. When they go under stress you have to do more spraying, so if you can keep them happy, you can grow more easily."

For gardens that cannot be watered regularly, spring-flowering bulbs and prairie plants provide more drought tolerance than gardens containing Eurasian species. Since most plants need adequate water to produce flowers, most gardens flower well in the spring. As the season progresses, many novice gardeners become discouraged, having not anticipated plants' need for water. The use of impatiens or lantana as indicator plants can help. When the indicator

Purple and white petunias in the container, with *Yucca filamentosa* and *Hosta plantaginea* 'Royal Standard'.

plants begin to wilt, the garden needs watering. Even the rudbeckia needs adequate moisture to maintain a full flowering effect and does not tolerate drought and hot dry winds. Since they thrive with little attention, prairie plants grow well where access to water is limited. Connor II says, "You can have flowers in the spring-time without watering, but you have to water if you want to have flowers summer through fall."

Finding the ideal location for any particular plant requires some experimenting. One area of the Shaws' garden is set aside for this purpose, a sort of laboratory for finding out how easily a plant adapts to the climate before placing it in the landscape. Plants receive protection from buildings and other plants. Giving delicate plants eastern exposure is more likely to assure hardiness for them than a western one.

The more tender the plant, the more attention should be paid to the exposure. The east side of the Shaws' house definitely stays wetter and does not get as cold as the north or west or as hot as the south or west sides. More moderate temperatures provide a better growing environment for most plants.

Spring-flowering bulbs and peo-

Coreopsis verticillata; Hemerocallis sp., baby's breath (Gypsophila paniculata); Coreopsis verticillata; blue spikes of Veronica longifolia; large candlelike, budding bottlebrush buckeye (Aesculus parviflora); Spirea x bumalda.

- *Plants native to the region adapt easily and beautifully to traditional designs.*
- *Consider the cultural requirements even of native plants before planting them. "Reading the land" assures growing healthy plants.*
- *Combine flowering shrubs with herbaceous perennials to produce a full effect all year.*
- *Create a natural grace by using trees and shrubs of different ages and sizes and planting them in clusters.*
- *Add a layer of compost each fall to improve soil texture and to promote winter hardiness.*
- *Pick the flowers of plants that self-sow easily to prevent them from taking over the garden.*
- *Use an indicator plant to help you tell when the garden needs watering.*
- *During a late-winter thaw, gently push shallow rooted plants that heave out of the ground back down with the heel of your shoe.*
- *Grow your roses along an eastern exposure to protect them from the extremes of the weather.*
- *A perennial garden takes three or four years to mature. Try to be patient.*

show of blooms. Shadier gardens near the house contain successful combinations thick with columbine, Virginia creeper, sweet woodruff, cranesbill, bellflowers, and a selection of ferns growing with such vigor that they look wild. For low, wet areas Siberian bugloss thrives (though it wouldn't survive in better-drained, raised beds). Microclimates even in one garden are important to identify.

Tucked at the edge near an entrance to a field, the Kentucky wisteria (*Wisteria macrostachya*) combines the color and form of the Japanese and Chinese wisterias with the hardiness the latter cannot match. This native species flowers after the leaves have appeared in early June with slightly shorter panicles of lavender blooms on sinuous, twining stems that wind gracefully up the fence for support. These hardy stems will not die back in winter and thrive much further north.

When Connor II plans the color for his garden, he has found that plants in the warm spectrum of red, yellow, and orange fit in the bright, sunny areas while the cooler blues and lavenders open and enhance the shady and semishady spots. The elder Connor emphasizes, "I like the hotter colors in the sun, but I don't choose the hot-colored orange impatiens in the shade; I'd rather choose white or pink." Outside the Shaws' bedroom window, the rose bed blooms, offering

the flowers' exquisite form and fragrance to those inside. The roses along the eastern side of the house receive the most protection possible, enabling the Shaws to enjoy the fragile plants without picking them. For more open, sunny spots polyantha roses like 'The Fairy' blend well

Flowering *Rudbeckia fulgida sullivanti* 'Gold-sturm' with the foliage of blue false indigo (*Baptisia australis*).

with the prairie dropseed grass and stachys. 'The Fairy' is more hardy and disease-resistant than 'Seafoam', another dwarf shrub rose growing nearby. Mixing the prairie with the European plants in this way tames the open spaces and adds vitality to the formal garden.

nies survive in exposed locations on the west side of the garden. With the lengthening days of spring, sunny, open locations encourage an early

Other than the prairie plants, the proven performers for the beginning gardener include daylilies, peonies, Siberian iris, and yarrow. Gardens develop with experience and require work and patience. Connor III stresses, "I don't think we're going to get people who have just a quasi-interest in gardening to do this because it does take work. Success is part of it, but to a true gardener, success and failure are all part of it. There's a transition that you go through as a gardener, and yet many are not willing to take a chance that some plants will not live. There is no iron-clad guarantee that every plant will live and flourish. This is not for people who want to plant it and walk away from it and hope like hell it's going to come off. Even then it's a five-year process to accomplish this; it didn't just happen in a year or two." His father adds, "Nothing is worse than to start a garden with a bunch of rare things and then have them die. Then you're nowhere. Delphiniums would be a mistake. First pick the things that are practical."

It takes several years for plants to mature and fill in. A green border like the Shaws' takes time as well as knowledge. Connor III uses similar but simpler designs for people who want to enjoy the beauty of a garden with the least amount of fuss. A perennial garden can take three to four years to mature, so he advocates putting a manageable garden where it can easily be viewed and enjoyed as it develops. "Our belief is if you do intensive landscaping, you do it up close to where you are all the time. The rest will turn woody to some degree. In the fall annuals look like dead plants, but many perennials look very nice all winter long."

Even using very hardy native plants, Connor III agrees with Penelope Hobhouse, who wrote, "The most difficult garden to design is an informal design and the most difficult garden to maintain is an informal garden." Connor elaborates, "If you put in a boxwood hedge with a ground cover under, then the only pruning is trimming and occasionally weeding; where if you go with an informal garden you're not dealing with just that. You go from just looking at it to gestalt—you have to know what you see."

Des Moines, Iowa

RUSSELL O'HARRA

In Russell O'Harra's backyard in Des Moines, Iowa, hostas abound. At one time his garden contained a wide range of perennial plants, but gradually his collection of hostas grew. Now his entire yard flourishes in a lush display of leaves and colors, and all the other plants are only subordinate companions. Although hostas are shade-loving plants, they grow easily over a wide range of conditions. Russ contends that the difficulty growing a variety of *Hosta* species and cultivars is "mainly just getting the right light. They need more light than what a lot of people say."

In the Midwest some hostas perform best when grown in part sun rather than deep shade. Russ refers to an area of heavy shade as an "absolutely dead corner" where "some will do all right, but some will just sit there and not do anything." Although some burn in too much light, most will not grow vigorously or at all if the light is too low. Pruning very shady spots lets in more light to stimulate growth. Filtered light in an area allows the gar-

den to accommodate many cultivars. Pruning trees as well as moving plants around positions each plant for the right amount of light.

Since hostas are not "heavy water users," they suit the growing conditions of much of the Midwest. Hostas

Hosta 'Fluctuans Variegated'.

can survive conditions of drought, but Russ notes, "They do 80 percent better if they're watered and fed occasionally. I usually give them a spring sprinkling of fertilizer, and that is it." In the fall soil mixes from the planters along the walk are dumped onto the garden as mulch to insulate the soil. The decaying peat moss and organic matter help enrich the soil the following spring. Amending even good soil improves drainage and fertility and stimulates plant growth.

Hostas are well suited to the midwestern soil and climate. Russ points out that in many areas "the soil pH is slightly alkaline and that's what hostas like." Yet even with the ten inches of topsoil with a suitable acidity, most of the garden is started with the technique of double digging. With this technique, the top layer of rich soil is removed and the lower clay subsoil level gets copious amounts of sand and peat moss. The richer topsoil goes into the bottom of the hole, and the amended subsoil fills in. In this way drainage and fertility improves to

Left: Large *Hosta* 'Ginko Craig'; purple garden heliotrope; in the background, a golden cultivar of *Hosta sieboldiana* 'Elegans'.

a depth of eighteen to twenty inches. Although this is "an exhausting amount of work," soil preparation is a very important part of growing plants successfully. Even though hostas grow well in the heavy, clay soils that cover most of the Midwest, care and attention prompts the best growth from the plants.

With this in mind, minimal maintenance requirements stand out as one of hostas' main advantages. Russ finds, "Weeding isn't any problem because hostas can shade any competition. Only every once in a while does a weed come up. In this country there must be five billion hostas. They face the shrub hedges; they line driveways. They're beautiful. They cut out all that trimming; you can just mow along. The leaves come out, and the mower just brushes by as it goes along."

Some varieties require dividing periodically. Noting when to dig them, Russ says, "The minute it folds down and doesn't make a solid stand, I get rid of it. If the stand gets a hole in the middle, I'll keep it, but I'll divide it." When the plant gets too old for foliage to arch gracefully outward from the crown, the process of dividing and renewal is necessary. However, for most hostas division is infrequent.

Slugs, the main pest problem of

Russ O'Harra's collection of more than forty new and older cultivars includes *Hosta* 'Shade Fanfare'.

hostas, feed hungrily on the foliage from the minute the new leaves emerge. Established stands of hostas, as well as newly planted specimens, suffer during cool, wet springs. When the plant's leaves fully mature and as the summer gets hotter and drier, the problem with slugs diminishes. Early in the spring, cleaning up all the protective mulch right down to the ground helps keep slugs under control. With the layers of mulch, Russ finds, "You're just providing the slugs with a beautiful home." Later in the summer as the weather becomes drier, returning the mulch helps conserve water.

In addition to good cultural practices, like the spring cleanup, he uses slug bait if the leaves start to show severe damage. The trick of carefully covering the bait with a saucer prevents birds from eating it. Like all pesticides, slug bait is a substance that should be used properly and only when the pest problem warrants it. Another creative solution to managing the pest population is by attracting birds. To attract these predators Russ says, "I throw bird seed late in the evening, and the birds eat anything that moves!" The birds become an additional feature as well as a garden worker.

The late-spring freezes common in the Midwest present the only other problem in growing hostas. Temperatures can drop below freezing as late as mid-May throughout the central

regions, let alone the northern areas of the Midwest. Each spring is slightly different from the one before. Russ proclaims enthusiastically, "One nice thing about hostas is they look marvelous when they come up in the spring, and they look good until frost. There are no other perennials that do that!" However, the spring weather that initiates this wonderful display can become a major problem when there are late-spring frosts.

Although the plants are not killed, some will be set back so much that they grow slowly for the entire season. Mulching the hostas with oak leaves, which do not decompose quickly, gives cover easily removed and occasionally easily reapplied with the warning of an impending frost. For composting, chopped leaves decay more quickly, but uncomposted leaves are easier

Here is a well-arranged collection of miniature hostas, including *Hosta* 'Golden Septre' and *Hosta* 'Butterana'.

to take off and put on. Russ smiles as he recalls the days when he collected oak leaves left in bags by neighbors at the edge of the street in his Cadillac!

In recent years, pine needles have replaced oak leaves as the preferred mulch. Pine needles are readily available in Russ's area, they don't become soggy and compacted, they allow

good drainage through them, the color blends well with the winter garden, they stay put and do not blow around, and they pull away from the crown of the plant easily. Also, fewer slugs crawl around in the needle bed than they do in the softer layers of leaves. Russ prefers pine needles to oak leaves, but he finds both will do the job.

Recalling one late frost, he remarks, "It took two days out of my life because I took all the mulch off, then we had a very late freeze. Fortunately, the frost was on a Friday night when all the neighbors' trash cans were empty. I just used trash cans over everything."

Although trash cans may seem unnecessarily large for covering emerging plants, a frost can occur after the leaves are almost fully grown and several of these plants are three feet tall. Timing is one of the biggest challenges to gardening here. Mulching is an important part of protection—even mulching with garbage cans.

Since hosta plants are often expensive, transplanting and dividing maintain their form and enlarge the garden. Usually a hosta takes three years to develop into a good specimen. Smaller cultivars that may reach only six inches mature faster than the giant three-foot plants. Some hostas grow so slowly and stay so compact that Russ admits "a lot of them I've never divided."

However, when they need to be separated, the best time to divide them is from late June until frost. When splitting the plants into large hunks, dividing them earlier, as they are first beginning to grow, works well. But Russ feels, "If you divide them into individual crowns, you should wait until they are well rooted. I wrecked one of my favorite plants because I dug it too early in the season. I have three little chunks of one expensive plant that still aren't doing anything." Having a well-developed, actively growing root system eases the shock of transplanting.

Although Russ does not have a master plan for his design, he varies the color, texture, and size in a graceful and appealing way, using masses of hostas in a gradual succession. In the center of one area a magnificent specimen of 'Sum and Substance' serves as a focal point with impressive three-foot golden leaves arching gracefully over the planting. Russ modestly describes his technique by saying, "I put a gold one, a green one, and a variegated one. There are so many choices; you have so many to work with you can do all sorts of

things." However, the natural transitions of size, form, and color in his garden produce a peaceful, unhurried, flowing feeling. Combining this natural grace that hostas produce with their season-long appeal, Russ's enthusiasm for growing an entire garden of hostas is easy to appreciate. He reminisces, "At one time I had 140 daffodils, but I can't stand the foliage. By June I would cut all their foliage off as it yellowed."

Some hosta flowers are also outstanding and fragrant, such as plantain lily (*Hosta plantaginea*) and *Hosta plantaginea* 'Royal Standard'. Still most of the flowers fall onto the foliage and become dried, like wallpaper. Since the texture, color, and form of the foliage is the focal point, removing the flowers becomes part of the maintenance.

Some of the new cultivars grow more slowly and with more difficulty than the old standards. Those developed and grown in test tubes on agar by a technique called tissue culture need special care. Even as small plants growing in two-to-four-inch pots they are delicate. Until they reach mature size or until they are "hardened off" in field soil, their root system needs the care of a nursery setting. Although tissue culture is a wonderful way to develop and propagate hostas, some plants not adapted to growing outside are hard to handle. After losing some new specimens of

'Northern Halo's Sunray', Russ advises buying sturdy plants to make gardening more dependable.

Even as new cultivars gain in popularity, old favorites like *Hosta helonioides* 'Albo-Picta' and the basic species like *Hosta lancifolia* are often easier to find and far less expensive. Russ finds some popular newer cultivars like 'Francis Williams' tend to burn and look unsightly and yet are still widely grown. Some, like 'Fascination', may be unstable and revert to a previous form. His best advice: "Buy from a reliable source and be prepared for some surprises. A sought-after plant at one Hosta Society meeting was 'Flamboyant', but it reverts to 'Shade Fanfare' and I love 'Shade Fanfare'. It seems that some don't come true out of the test tube, where they are full of some hormones. It takes them a year to show what they're going to be. My straight 'Nigrescens' isn't 'Nigrescens' at all, which I'm delighted with because I like it a lot better!"

As a gardener who specializes in hostas, Russ considers growing new and interesting forms an adventure. Available from some specialty growers, unnamed tissue-culture sports provide a challenge. Without knowing what might finally develop, new plants take a spot in the garden. Even from one mature stand, a side clump,

Right: Hosta 'White Christmas' light a circle of impatiens.

looking totally unlike the parent plant, sometimes sprouts. Sometimes these "sports" become new, prized cultivars. Russ says, "It just happens that's how many marvelous plants get started. That's the master sport of them all—'Sun Power'."

Although Russ's interest in hostas began while he was garden editor of *Better Homes and Gardens*, he remembers that his mother had a large garden and grew seven of the eleven available hostas at that time. He notes, "What my mother had were all straight species. Sixty years ago when she was gardening there were no cultivars. In fact having as many as she did made her a collector. Much later I remember being asked by one hosta enthusiast for some information on hosta sources. When I saw his hostas, I just went crazy. People get a very fast obsession. I always give little starter kits to visitors, and within two or three years they just have to have all of them!"

In addition to all the hostas, many interesting companion plants like ferns, houseplants, and shade-loving annuals highlight the garden. With its attractive coloration and finely articulated margins, the Japanese painted fern combines beautifully. Tropical houseplants arranged in the garden lend a lush, exotic appeal. Pots of large African violets and cape prim-

Hosta 'Grimes Golden' and tuberous begonia.

roses dug into the soil bloom naturally along the path. Pieces of baby's tears planted directly into the ground spread like a fine green carpet among the plants. A peperomia near a miniature hosta like 'Tiny Tears' adds a slight contrast in form and composition. Houseplants fit in so nicely and grow so well that only one pot saved over winter starts the garden in the following spring.

Hostas are as dependable, carefree, varied, and attractive as any perennial. Even the fall color of hostas like 'Vanette' round out the season with a subtle elegance. Enthusiasm for them is catching. As Russ says, "They look marvelous when they first come up, and they look marvelous when the frost hits them. There are so many choices, you can do all sorts of things with them. Even casual gardeners find they soon want to collect them all." These simple plants once kept to ring trees and line driveways now comprise an enormous group that produces stunning displays. Once the supporting players, hostas have become stars of the garden.

Hosta sieboldiana 'Elegans'.

- *Dump the soil mixes from planters into the garden in late fall to serve as a mulch and improve the texture and fertility of the soil.*

- *Hostas actually grow in a range of light intensities.*

- *Divide hostas when they lose their umbrellalike form to help maintain their elegant shape and multiply your collection.*

- *Keep the spring garden free of mulch to help prevent infestations of slugs.*

- *Have some kind of quick cover handy for late spring frosts.*

- *Pine needles and uncomposted large leaves give good winter and early spring cover for the plants.*

- *Although some flowers are outstanding, removing the flowers prevents petals from sticking to the leaves like wallpaper.*

- *Mature plants are easier for the amateur to grow than seedlings or plants newly transplanted out of tissue culture tubes.*

- *Ferns, house plants, and shade-loving annuals are all good companions for hostas.*

Bald Eagle, Minnesota

LOIS CARLSON

The garden of Lois Carlson in Bald Eagle, Minnesota, exhibits energy and color during the long, sunny summer days of the Upper Midwest despite the wintery blasts that have come before. A period of light snow and strong winds prevent many zone 4 plants from surviving. (Without hesitation Lois asserts, "No matter what they say, this is zone 3. All you have to have is one night where the temperature plunges below thirty degrees Fahrenheit with no snow cover to kill many supposedly hardy plants.") More interesting than what does not survive the rigors of the region are the glorious results she achieves regardless of the climatic extremes.

The key to winter hardiness in the northern garden is snow cover. Without adequate insulation, chrysanthemums and roses are about the first plants to die out. However, in the loose soil during years when a twelve-inch blanket of snow insulates the mums by Thanksgiving, they not only survive, they grow. With a good layer of snow as insulation all winter, a planting of mums may be larger in the spring than in the fall.

Learning the techniques of northern gardening came early to Lois's family, who produced an extensive vegetable garden. When she was about ten, she convinced her parents to let her order some flower seeds out of a catalog. Her first perennials were a collection of irises. "I remember when I was in college, I ordered some irises out of a catalog. I got sixty varieties and paid for them myself. They sent two of each, and all I remember when I planted them is that my mother said,

Coleus 'Rainbow' hybrid mix; pink polka dot plant (*Hypoestes phyllostachya* 'Pink Splash'); and *Sedum* sp.

Left: Impatiens burst from pots (on the left) and from the ground (on the right).

'There goes another row of corn.' When I married and moved here, I brought the irises with me, which are now in the back garden."

In the beginning the garden contained only several hundred tulips strung in a narrow twelve-inch-wide border along the back fence. Each year the lawn gave up a little more to the advancing flowers. Thousands of plants growing there came slowly over the last fourteen years. In addition to the many perennials, Lois now rounds out the garden with ten thousand coleus and twelve thousand impatiens producing a spectacular show. Lois notes, "It's probably been this way for about four years. I'm not going to widen it anymore because I don't have enough room to grow everything for it."

Only when irises lack a sunny location do they easily succumb to borers and rots. "You've got to give them the right site for them to have a chance anyway," Lois emphasizes. Among the irises, the dark blue Siberian 'Eagle' and the lighter blue Siberian 'Super Eagle' give sturdy attractive displays, flowering until the end of June. Their foliage becomes an attractive complement to the nearby geraniums later in the summer. The small bright blooms of *Dianthus deltoides* 'Zing Rose' spread slowly through the garden, giving bursts of

Pots of coleus and impatiens with alyssum planted at the foot of the stairs.

color from a low mat of narrow-leafed foliage. They flower with the Siberians and bring out the blues very well.

With the earliest iris, the creeping phlox (*Phlox subulata*) 'Emerald Pink', begins the spectacular show. Later, the tight mat of bright green foliage serves as an outstanding ground cover for the entire summer. At the edge, between the lawn and the bed, the phlox grows along a dike of soils slightly raised above the level of the lawn. The change in height between the border and the lawn prevents the grass from growing over the top and smothering out the phlox. As Lois points out, "If you keep it at ground level, the grass can easily grow over the top of it."

One key to transplanting *Phlox subulata* successfully is to do so right after flowering. Second, keep the plants well watered until they become established. Finally, although a variety of sedums will hold onto the soil as it washes out from between the rocks in the shady rock garden, creeping phlox will not persist in areas subject to erosion, frequent drying, or shade.

Pieces of an old concrete driveway, laboriously pounded out and discarded, form the wall of the rock garden. The rough texture of exposed aggregate creates an interesting background for the sedums growing among them. The resulting raised, shady bed grows a variety of plants, including a pale pink monarda, and

the native, pale blue wildflower, Jacob's ladder.

A perennial performer, the rosy lavender spikes of *Stachys grandiflora* 'Big Betony' grow easily near the irises, picking up the color in the bed as the tall beardeds finish. The wrinkly, heart-shaped leaves contrast well with the finer *Phlox subulata* 'Emerald

Siberian iris 'Super Eagle'.

Jewels' in front and the stately iris straps in back. The sandy, well-drained soil provides it with a perfect home, and Lois remarks, "It's a wonderful perennial. With it I have color here all the time and I don't have to do anything to it. Within three years I

was able to divide my original one plant into thirteen new ones."

Later in the season interplanting the irises with annuals hides the foliage as it browns and fades. Remembering how she began the technique of putting pots of annuals among the perennials, Lois notes, "If you're not spraying constantly, they get leaf spot—you know, the little circles that widen—I hated it. I started to plant in between by putting pots in there. By late July you don't even recognize the garden. I like the annuals very much for summer color."

A limiting factor in the garden is the shade. The most colorful summer perennials grow best in full sun. The garden does not have enough sun for a showy display of perennials during July and August. However, the perennials that do perform well at the end of the shady setting include the stately, five-foot *Filipendula rubra* (queen of the prairie), whose pale pink plumes float like clouds above the lush fine-textured growth. *Ligularia przewalskii* 'Golden Candles' and pots of *Lythrum salicaria* 'Morden's Pink' grow tall, adding shafts of color to the thick growth of ferns. To slow the thick, rhizomatous growth, the lythrum stays in large five-gallon pots dug into the loose soil. Nearby *Malva sylvestris* remains hardy as well as slowly spreading by seeds. These small hollyhocklike flowers blend well with the light, airy tamarax, which comes up from the ground each year. Mixed in this area, *Echinacea purpurea* (purple coneflowers), *Liatris spicata*, and *Chelone glabra* (turtlehead), thrive in the light shade and loamy sand enriched by years of adding organic matter.

A raised walkway made from parts of an old deck separates the wild garden from the more formal displays of annuals. To allow access from the walk, a path of stepping stones winds into the area. Bordered by a row of amur maples, the mixture of self-seeding annuals and perennials changes only slightly each year. During severe winters even many resilient perennials will die out. For that reason, self-seeding annuals like *Chrysanthemum parthenium* (matricaria or fever few), *Cleome* (spider flower), and *Silene vulgaris* (bladder campion), replace them. Although many tall, elegant lupines die during hard winters, they will survive and spread easily by seeds in areas that are well drained and rich in organic material.

Amending this sandy soil takes time. When Lois's garden began, many yards of black dirt were added to enrich the soil, allowing a wide range of plants to thrive. Now each fall all of the mix from the hundreds of potted annuals are dumped into the beds. This layer of peat moss, perlite, and vermiculite serves as a winter mulch as well as organic matter for the garden. Regardless of the quality of the soil, constant addition of organic matter improves its texture and fertility for both perennials and annuals.

Not only do annuals produce tremendously colorful summers and provide a way to cover waning perennial foliage, in many ways they are no more work or expense than the perennials. Lois points out, "People say

Japanese painted fern (*Athyrium goeringianum* 'Pictum'); deep rose double impatiens; pink petunias; and pink musk mallows (*Malva moschata*).

'Plant perennials. They come back; no problem; no work.' They are a lot of work. Don't let anyone fool you. The only one I don't have to do anything to is that *Salvia pratensis*. It has a long spike of dark blue flowers. I've tried 101 different things under this over-hang. It gets no rain unless it blows in. I have to water it by hand, but it loves it in there. Still, after flowering, I cut it back and I divide it every few years. The hostas, ferns, and sedums also are good, but the hostas can get slug damage." Both annuals and perennials require care and attention.

The pink salvia 'Clarissa' reseeds easily and gives a dependable display in July near the pale pink monarda. However, an invading annual, the *Silene* 'Crimson Campion' seeds so rampantly that few other seeding annuals can match its aggressiveness. When not controlled, the bright, single rose flower pushes out cleome and *Amaranthus* 'Pigmy Torch'. As Lois says, "It's a very pretty flower. I like the color; that's why I left some of it. The combination of it with the rosy monarda and the orchid-red and rose-pink impatiens and lavender cleome gave this the label of a 'Mauve Garden.' But the *Silene* is crowding everything and doesn't even bloom well when there are so many of them. They have become a real problem. Nothing is this aggressive. I'm not sure I'm willing to keep them."

Even the attractive combination of *Oenothera fruticosa* youngii (four o'clocks or sundrops), and *Campanula glomerata*, with its pale yellow and blue complement, fade when the *Oenothera* overrun the *Campanula*, choking them out.

Controlling the balance of a perennial garden becomes another task overlooked by the beginning gardener, who may have difficulty thinking of beautiful flowers as weeds. For perennial weeds whose roots and rhizomes burrow through from outside the garden, a creative response includes burying a plastic barrier along a fence line. This blocks the assault of weeds like heal-all and lamb's quarter. With the plastic in a strip two feet deep, only weeds sprouting from seeds carried in need to be continually attacked.

Each fall Lois takes cuttings from the impatiens and coleus and keeps them over winter for the next year's garden. She cuts off the top three to four inches of the plants and sticks them into two-inch pots containing a growing mixture of milled peat moss, perlite, and vermiculite. All winter thousands of cuttings grow under lights in the basement. By overwintering fifteen thousand coleus, represented by 125 varieties, as well as ten thousand impatiens, Lois maintains a garden twelve months a year. The garden simply moves underground and under lights, keeping the thread of growth going during the dark, cold days of winter.

Lois admits, "When I started I didn't know how to take a cutting. I cut the whole thing to the ground and stuck them in a five-quart ice-cream pail and watched them rot. Then I cut the tops off and put them in little cups with tin foil on top and later transferred them to potting soil. Many of them died. Later I joined a garden club, and they said 'Don't root in water; put them in this peat moss mix.' There they all wilted until I finally found I had to put them under plastic. Only geraniums like it on the dry side." Now with a rigid regime of

Lilium 'Stargazer'; high mallow (*Malva sylvestris*); and blue salvia.

water, lighting, and fertilizing coupled with careful cleaning, bleaching, and sorting containers, the garden keeps going all winter.

New impatiens seeds replace any cuttings that die from disease or cultural problems. For several years the

impatiens became distorted by late winter, and many died. One problem can be traced to a faulty gas valve but also a virus carried by thrips may attack impatiens grown inside during the winter. When problems overwintering annuals arise, new plants are started from seeds. Growing annuals in this way gives plants that have fewer side branches. Then the tall seedlings are placed very close together in the garden, on three-inch centers, to force as much height out of them as possible. This produces a tall display of flowers behind which grow a row of impatiens planted in five-gallon plastic pots. The plants in front grow up and completely cover the pots, giving the effect of a wall of flowers. A bank of flowers over three feet tall starts at the edge of the lawn and stretches nearly to the top of the fence surrounding the yard.

In addition to annuals, roses also grow in pots. Lois does not use the Minnesota Tip to overwinter the roses. The Minnesota Tip consists of digging a trench next to the rose and tipping the entire plant on its side and burying it with two or three feet of soil. Growing roses in pots and burying the whole thing furnishes another method of overwintering roses in the harsh climate. In the spring transplanting the entire plant in new soil mix helps stimulate growth.

Growing plants in pots not only gives extra height to the garden but

Variegated impatiens; mixed varieties of coleus in pots; and in the background, more impatiens.

quickly draining sandy soil. If allowed to dry out, like a sponge, the peat mixture will not easily take up water. For that reason the plants in pots must be monitored carefully and cannot be left unattended for many days during the summer.

Around the garden, pots of Peruvian daffodils and elegant calla lilies accompany the more typical show of geraniums. Lois smiles, pointing to a calla lily, patiently tended from seed for five years. "I'm excited about that. You get one thing now and then that finally works. I've become known as the pot lady. It doesn't matter what it is. These are my dahlias. They don't go in the ground anymore. A gopher got them when they were planted in the ground. Next the tulips are going in pots. You've got to have them up front when they're flowering, but when they die down, I want them in the back so you don't have to see the dead leaves."

Asiatic and regal lilies thrive in the well-drained soils. However, one year gophers ate all except a few small lilies, requiring a creative approach to culture. Here again planting in pots came in handy. Planted in five-gallon containers and buried in the ground, the bulbs lived through the winter; the gophers couldn't touch them.

Azaleas and rhododendrons perform well and give a flash of color to the emerging garden. PJM rhododendrons and Northern Lights azaleas are the choice of the harsh climate. The deciduous Northern Lights come in various shades of white, pink, and golden yellow. The clusters of one- to one-and-a-half-inch fragrant flowers grow on compact shrubs that reach six to seven feet and survive temperatures of minus forty-five degrees Fahrenheit. Two months later the clematis 'Silver Moon' shines with large, iridescent pale blue flowers from under the shade of the nearby trees. As a dependable cover along the front fence, it greets visitors to the garden.

All this beauty came slowly. As Lois reassures any new gardener, "Most of gardening is trial and error. If you want a plant badly enough, you're going to try it. I've tried

also allows the design to be easily changed. The plants in pots must be watered more regularly than those planted in the ground. However, pots dug into the soil will hold water very well since the native, sandy soil dries out so quickly. Three days of hot, dry weather will dry the lawn to such an extent that the areas will die out. The pots actually hold water like a sponge compared to the coarse-textured,

- *A thick layer of snow provides the best winter protection for the garden.*
- *Annuals offer brilliant and dependable summer color in the coldest regions of the country.*
- *Grow bearded and Siberian iris in well-drained sunny locations, where they will more successfully withstand the devastation of iris borer.*
- *Clumps of the narrow-arching leaves of Siberian iris complement the late-summer garden.*
- *Grow creeping phlox (Phlox subulata), slightly above the elevation of the lawn to slow the invasion of turf grass rhizomes.*
- *Assemble chunks of discarded concrete into a retaining wall to provide an economical and natural-looking substitute for quarried stone.*
- *Each fall, take cuttings of annuals like coleus and impatiens to provide an abundant supply for the next year.*
- *Place pots of annuals among the early-spring perennials to hide the fading foliage.*
- *Each fall, dump pots of peat, perlite, and vermiculite mixture from the annual displays into your garden to add a valuable layer of winter insulation and to enrich the soil.*
- *Beware of annuals that self-sow easily. They may become a weed and choke out less aggressive plants.*
- *To slow weeds traveling by rhizomes or roots into the garden from neighboring areas, try burying a plastic barrier along a fence line.*
- *Grow your roses in containers all summer, and it will be easy to bury them for winter protection.*
- *Carefully monitor the plants you grow in containers, to prevent them from drying out.*

Purple coneflower (*Echinacea purpurea*); impatiens and salvia in front; pots of impatiens in back.

things twice, putting them in different areas. It's so encouraging when you see something blooming. I've got to have a few perennials come out so I can get myself going. It's so therapeutic. I find after a long winter, I can't wait to get out and start working in the garden. But don't start gardening on a big scale. You'll be disappointed."

Lois Carlson's energy is outshined only by her patience, for which she is rewarded. Her steady effort blooms each year in an abundance of color.

Wilmette, Illinois

THOMAS AND HÉLÈNE JAMES

At home in her garden five blocks from Lake Michigan, just north of Chicago, Hélène James reveals, "My husband and I like planting things that are not commonly used. The Midwest can have as beautiful and interesting a garden as anywhere. There are so many plants that are not used or offered in nurseries. I enjoy the beauty of a garden, and I enjoy the research and work that goes along with making one."

Mature trees and evergreens comprise the background for perennials and old shrub roses in the Jameses' yard. During a trip to England, Hélène and her husband Thomas visited the large rose collection at Mottisfont Abbey. The unusual gardens brought to their peak by the renowned rosarian, Graham Stuart Thomas, inspired their garden. As Hélène remembers, Thomas "fell in love" with the antique shrub roses growing there. "I could not stop it. He had to have them." As a result, over the last few years their quiet North Shore landscape began to explode with a collection of more than twenty varieties of old shrub roses arranged in large sweeping beds.

After their visit to the English gar-

Climbing hydrangea (*Hydrangea anomala petiolaris*); variegated hosta; annual blue salvia; yellow pansies; pink moss shrub rose 'William Lobb'.

dens, Thomas and Hélène began planning a garden for Illinois by reading about roses' hardiness and care. As ideas for the garden crystallized, books such as *Classic Roses* by Peter Beales went with them on vacation. Their main concern was selecting plants that could withstand the brutal midwestern winters as well as the often sweltering summers.

Out of this concern for hardiness, the Jameses chose to purchase their plants from a northern nursery specializing in shrub roses, the Pickering Nursery in Pickering, Ontario, near Toronto. After all, Toronto has a climate no less severe than Wilmette's. Hélène recognizes there are other nurseries but explains, "If they are raised in Canada, they have more chance to adapt to our weather."

Fortunately, the Jameses' garden is near a large body of water and suffers less from the wild temperature swings common to much of the region. The "lake effect" gives the garden warmer winters and cooler summers than gar-

Left: Forget-me-not (*Myosotis alpestris* 'Victoria'); *Coreopsis lanceolata*; *Geranium endressii* 'Wargrave Pink'; perennial blue salvia (*Salvia* x *superba* 'East Friesland'); *Astrantia major* ; Pink Gallica Rose 'Belle de Crecy'.

dens just thirty miles farther west. The water soaks up the summer heat like a sponge to slowly let it back out again during the winter. Even so, one climbing rose of their extensive collection, the lovely, fragrant, soft pink 'Mme. Alfred Carriere', did not thrive in spite of its reputation for standing up to northern exposures. As important as research is, the ultimate test is trying out the plant in one's own garden.

After Hélène and Thomas selected plants based on hardiness, their plan evolved around the use of shades of pinks in the back bed with the more striking reds, lavenders, and whites in the front. The tall elms provide mottled shade for the beds, which are positioned to take advantage of the pockets of light coming through the mature canopy.

Hosta sieboldiana 'Elegans' and *Thalictrum adiantifolium*.

Preparing the soil becomes as important as choosing the roses and positioning the beds. The fine-textured clay slows root growth. Puddles around the plants smother delicate roots that need air to survive. Bags of peat moss in the clay soil lighten the texture and let roots and shovels penetrate easily, allowing water to drain more efficiently. Along with the peat, bone meal encourages the roots to become established in their new surroundings.

In the winter an added layer of organic matter, usually mushroom compost, piled about one to two feet around the base of the plants, gives them a layer of insulation. When there is little or no snow cover, the layer of winter mulch helps mediate the swings in temperature. The lightweight compost goes on easily and just as easily spreads over the soil during the growing season. In the spring, pulling the mulch away from the base of the plant and leveling it throughout the beds holds down weeds and keeps the soil cool.

Most of the plants bloom only once, in June, and need only minimal care. Early in the spring any dieback is cut away to improve appearance and vigor. After flowering, all of the faded blossoms are removed to encourage vegetative growth and discourage any diseases harbored by the decaying flowers. The plants look much neater cleared of the dead flowers. Since some plants, like the Apothecary's Rose, (*Rosa gallica officinalis*), have attractive hips, some are left. Only when the plants become leggy and open does any further pruning need to be done, and this only every few years when straggly growth habits dictate.

The plants can be put into the ground in spring or late fall. The roses need fertilizing to flourish; a slow-release fertilizer reduces the amount of work in that regard. Other than this minimal care and the obligatory cleanup of any blotchy, diseased foliage, the roses take care of themselves. As Hélène affirms, "I don't spray them. We have too many and I really don't like using sprays. We did at first, but we stopped and I don't think they are less healthy for it."

Although the roses are now the focal point of the garden, over ten years ago Hélène began with two planting beds along the front walk. As she and Thomas became interested in tree peonies and roses, the gardens grew. "I started with a few pots and then these two beds," she remembers. "My husband became interested in tree peonies, so we had to have a bed for the tree peonies. Then we bought the roses so we had to have a bed for the roses." Along with these, spring bulbs and summer perennials fill out the display.

Tucked behind some larger plants in the front garden, the lenten rose (*Helleborus*) thrives early in the spring. Later the blues of the forget-me-nots (*Myosotis sylvatica*), the tiny colorful Johnny-jump-ups (*Viola tricolor*), along with the richly colored pansies blanket the bed. Here the radiant moss shrub rose 'William Lobb' blooms with large fragrant clusters of semidouble flowers. Catching the attention of visitors, this rose's unusual color varies from purple to pink with a light silver cast underneath and gets the characteristic name 'Moss Rose' (*Rosa* x *centifolia* 'Muscosa') from the fuzzy texture of its buds and stems. Behind this combination of deep blues and rosy reds, the deep green leaves and velvety pink flowers of 'Fantin Latour' cast a spell.

As the season progresses, the roses give way to a mixture of perennials arranged around the arching canes. Near the front walk, a full stand of the delicate round, starlike spheres of the flowers of *Astrantia major* catch the sun pouring into the holes of the tall canopy of trees. They are long flowering plants whose small, delicate blossoms hold well when cut.

July finds pale pink plumes of *Filipendula rubra* (queen of the prairie) waving elegantly over the garden. A mixture of late-blooming phlox gives color and depth to the summer beds as the thick, long-lasting *Nepeta mussinii* (catmint) ties the bed to the ground.

During the life of any garden, new plants come and less desirable ones are removed. The tall, gray foliage and the late summer, light blue flow-

Rose *R.* x *centifolia* 'Fantin Latour'; catmint (*Nepeta x faassenii*); Coreopsis behind.

ering cloud of *Perovskia atriplicifolia* (Russian sage) become a new backdrop for the garden, while the invasive, bright yellow *Heliopsis helianthoides* 'Summer Sun' false sunflower, overpowers the location and must be removed.

In a garden already rich with stately dominating roses, lythrum and goldenrod also become too competitive. The large, torchlike *Lythrum* competes for space in the limited areas with the graceful candles and round rhythmic leaves of *Ligularia*. Even in protected sites, and cooled by the lake's breezes, the *Ligularia* still wilts during the hot, midsummer afternoons. Only in moist soil and nearly complete shade will it survive.

By late summer the nasturtiums growing along the walk replace the pansies with shades of orange and yellow. Each spring a few seeds sprinkled at the edge of the bed sprout, nearly covering the front walk by fall. As the season comes to an end, the mums, sedums, asters, and nasturtiums put on the final act. With these traditional late-summer choices, the tufted hair grass *Deschampsia caespitosa* waves its clumps of low, thin arching leaves and misty, ethereal flowers from June until August.

For the most part, climbing roses grow here without additional protection. Occasionally some do die back

Bourbon rose—'Madame Isaac Pereire'.

to the ground, like the large lavender and pink flowered Bourbon rose 'Mme. Isaac Pereire' climbing along the front fence. As the parkway trees mature and produce more shade to the front of the garden, the elegantly rambling 'Mme. Isaac Pereire' changes also. Although it receives less direct light, the plant continues to grow and bloom. But its strength declines because during severe cold spells, more canes die back to the ground. Growing very slowly at first, the climbing hydrangea (*Hydrangea anomala petiolaris*) thrives and blooms along the fence, with large open clusters on top of shiny, dark green leaves. This garden is never static. The plants evolve together—some becoming more vigorous with the changes, some becoming less.

The bright yellow flowers of the shrub *Kerria japonica* and the deep violet clusters on the compact Meyer lilac (*Syringa meyeri*) combine with clumps of pink tulips and dark blue bachelor's buttons and irises to start the colorful front border. Later the eye-catching roses 'Tuscany' and 'Tuscany Superb', two deep red, semi-double gallica roses with velvety petals and compact forms, bloom with the lively white damask, 'Mme. Hardy', and the distinctive white rugosa 'Blanc Double de Coubert'. The roses all are very hardy and blend into the shrub border with compact form, interesting texture, and even attractive fall color. Adding depth and contrast during July, *Malva alcea Fastigiata* bloom with tiny hollyhock-like flowers in shades of pink and lavender accompanied by Lady's Mantle (*Alchemilla mollis*), whose distinctive round, chartreuse-gray leaves bead with jewellike drops of dew each morning. Its yellow-green flowers add mass, and a light outlines the form of the bed. In the fall the pink showy stonecrop *Sedum spectabilis* carries the soft, warm tones through the garden.

Muted grays and clear blues blend well with the lovely spectrum of pinks in the back garden. 'Koenigin von Daenemark' (The Queen of Denmark), a pale regal pink; 'General Kleber', a moss rose with bright green, full foliage and dainty pink flowers; 'Reine des Violettes', a fragrant hybrid perpetual, whose leaves carry a musky, lingering scent when bruised; and the

Lady's mantle (*Alchemilla mollis*); roses *Rosa gallica* 'Tuscany' and 'Tuscany Superb'.

ancient 'Rosa Mundi' (*R. gallica* 'Versicolor'), a bicolor named for the mistress of King Henry II of England more than eight hundred years ago, combine in a bed circling the delicate spires of clear blue delphiniums, breaking the wind.

Since only 20 to 25 percent of the delphiniums are coaxed through the winter, the stately, elegant plants are added each year. Also, since the fine-textured, silver globes of *Artemesia schmidtiana* 'Silver Mound' only survive the winter in very well-drained soil, each spring they are newly planted. As Hélène admits, "I've tried to plant a nice collection of perennials to go with the roses. But many don't come back. I don't get discouraged; I just replace them or try something else. I like *Campanula* with roses, but they don't do well here. I think the catmints (*Nepeta mussinii*) are good and some of the geraniums."

The more dependable, flowerless cultivar of lamb's ear (*Stachys byzantina* 'Silver Carpet') produces a perennial blanket at the edge of the beds. Six-to-eight-foot towers of lavender and blue clematis join the spirited, large white clematis 'Henryi' growing on supports in the beds. The bright *Dianthus* sp. with deep rose flowers on a gray-green mat carry the pink color to the edge of the garden. With the dependable light blue catmint (*Nepeta* sp.), several species of the perennial blue veronicas give contrasting color.

- *Northern-grown stock provides plants more adapted to the harsh midwestern climate.*
- *Place beds in the pockets of light shining down through the trees' mature canopy of leaves to allow roses and trees in the same garden.*
- *Mix ample amounts of peat moss and bone meal into the soil when you plant, to lighten and enrich the clay soil.*
- *Pile organic matter, preferably mushroom compost, one or two feet over the plants in late autumn to help insulate plants against rapid fluctuations of winter temperatures.*
- *Remove faded flowers to discourage diseases promoted by decaying petals and to produce a neater-looking plant.*
- *Leave flowers on plants with attractive, long-lived hips.*
- *When plants become leggy and open, prune them to encourage new, compact growth.*
- *Use a slow-release fertilizer on roses to reduce maintenance.*
- *Clean out any blotchy, diseased foliage to keep the plant healthy.*
- *Mix seeds of various lettuces together in one area to produce a variety for salads, as well as an interesting garden.*
- *An old ladder buried in the ground makes ideal planting "boxes" for aggressive plants like mints and monarda.*

'Fantin Latour' with sundrops (*Oenothera tetragona*).

The magnificently full, pink cabbage form of 'Fantin Latour' beside the slightly darker, ancient Apothecary's Rose (*R. gallica officinalis*) stands near the back door, by the herb and vegetable garden. The Apothecary's Rose, grown for use in teas and remedies in the Middle Ages, is one of the oldest roses in cultivation. Still, it holds firm as a beautiful addition to the garden with its single, clear, deep rose-colored flowers and heady fragrance.

Next to the garage another large, spreading 'Fantin Latour' stands with the tall, light yellow native sundrops (*Oenothera tetragona*) as a companion. The combination of the native American with the French aristocrat lends a fresh look to two ancients from different worlds.

In the vegetable garden the French custom of combining varieties of lettuce in one planting area becomes a useful technique to save space as well as an attractive use of the many colors and textures of different lettuces. The garden looks like a salad tossed elegantly on a grand scale.

Mesclum, the planting technique that combines a mixture of seeds in one area, makes growing vegetables a visual art as well as a space saver. An old, creaky ladder makes an ingenious frame for the raised bed. The mints, basils, and monarda stay in their own "rung," mixing the formal look of geometry with the creative use of an old ladder.

Along the north side of the house, the moist shady soil grows *Brunnera* with large heart-shaped leaves whose masses of tiny blue flowers come early in the spring. Mixed in this setting are two cultivars of the crinkly-leafed *Bergenia*, the unusual nodding trillium and bright yellow primrose. A path leads to a lovely old beech whose roots find enough loose soil to grow as a strong, stately specimen. Though slightly north of its range, the temperate strip of land easily provides a happy situation to this climax forest tree from a few hundred miles south. Under its dense shade, *Pachysandra* and periwinkle mix together as one ground cover, blending their leaves in an interesting tapestry of color and form.

Although the entire garden produces highlights throughout the year, in June shrub roses hold the perennial garden in hypnotic splendor. The graceful arching branches dotted in some cases and covered in others with the many forms and colors of roses—some unchanged since they were developed hundreds of years ago—cast a special spell on the garden.

Looking at roses named after ancient kings and lovers transports Hélène and Thomas and their visitors to another time and a different world. These plants are garden aristocrats showing their grace and elegance in a well-planned perennial display. They may hold court only once a season, so like many other perennials, the length of their blooming period does not justify them. Their value lies in their beauty.

'Tuscany' with deep blue spiderwort (*Tradescantia virginiana*).

Northern Michigan

HOWARD COBB

Driving north along Route 119 from Harbor Springs, Michigan, the thick woods lining the road open slightly to reveal a glimpse of color and bloom usually reserved for tamer scenery farther south. Near the forests used for hiking and hunting, a native Kentuckian returns each spring to garden in the luxury of the crisp, fresh air, the light, sandy soil, and the bright, clear skies of northern Michigan.

Nearly seventy years ago Howard Cobb's family brought Howard's frail infant brother north to escape the heavy, humid air and sweltering conditions of the southeastern summers. The annual migration continues for many members of his family, but only Howard paints an opening in the woods that resem-

'Enchantment' lilies with golden marguerite daisies (*Anthemis sancti-johannis*).

bles a genteel, southern scene. This blending of North and South culminates in the varied texture of Howard's version of a midwestern garden.

Two large rectangular beds flank the front woods and grab the eye. Changing patterns of perennials fill the beds with brilliant color, which is set off by the dark green evergreens and white-barked birches. At the far end of this northern retreat, between the two lines of flowers, waits a white wooden bench. The beds edged with brick and the white bench further provoke the feeling of a southern garden moved north. The sound of the lake beyond the line of trees brings a hypnotic lull to the garden. When the early morning mist rolls in, the restful bench, blanketed in fog and surround-

Left: Foxgloves (*Digitalis purpurea*); English wallflower (*Cheiranthus cheiri*); with marguerite and shasta daisies.

ed by flowers, becomes bathed in light. Here the quiet gardener can rest, view the plants at eye level, and become part of the congregation of living things.

Patches of light filter into the woods where naturalized Asiatic lilies mix red and yellow with the green of midsummer. The long days and intense light of the northern zone provide an equivalent of four hours of direct light needed for them to bloom. By opening the forest slightly, just enough light comes in to coax flowers. Only the deer, roaming in abundance and eating the flower buds, curb the show.

This garden started as a field of sumac and very rocky soil. Howard recalls its beginning: "My original garden wasn't where it is now. It was just a background garden with the arborvitae hedge behind. Every year I extended it, until now I can't go any farther. But I've got a path through the wood, and there I'm having fun experimenting with green things that like shade. We arrive the first of May, and the floor is just carpeted with trillium and acres of myrtle. Things like that do so well here. But don't think we do as well with tulips as they do in southern Michigan. The deer and rabbits constantly eat them."

The deer also favor roses, helianthus, and hollyhocks, so they're becoming a considerable predator. And in winter as the snow covers the forest floor, their foraging becomes even more serious. Unabated, they clip the arborvitae hedge that runs along the side garden. However, during the summer the techniques used to discourage them range from rags soaked with deer repellant hanging from sticks placed throughout the beds to simply running into the garden and shooing them away.

Phlox maculata 'Alpha'; shasta daisy; *Heliopsis helianthoides* 'Summer Sun'.

Like rabbits with bigger appetites and longer legs, deer won't hesitate to eat almost any perennial. Growing a garden with such wildlife pressures takes persistence and ingenuity. A new gardener will learn the disappointment of seeing not just an expensive plant become fodder but the pang of loss at a promising bud vanishing unfulfilled. All gardeners find chipmunks, squirrels, rabbits, and deer worthy opponents able to bring the garden to its knees (or rather, its stems). The historical "hordes of locust" vanquishing the land bring visions of farmers beating the flying swarms in futile struggles. The modern gardener experiences troubles dating back to the beginning of cultivation. What a tie to the past! And what hope for the future. To outwit four-legged predators should be looked on not as a burden but a privilege of living in a complex world. A garden becomes a place to interact with the real web of life on this planet.

The garden began as a vegetable garden, but today many fine sources of fresh summer produce are available. (Predators to a vegetable garden are even more intent than in a flower garden.) A remnant of the original vegetable garden remains with the large, dark green leaves of rhubarb, which contribute gentle, wavy margins, adding fullness to the garden. Howard says, "It's lovely in the garden, and I love it too."

Any midwestern perennial display changes almost weekly. The sometimes not-so-subtle changes in weather bring to mind the movements of a symphony. The cadenza comes not to a final climax and resolution but like a

Naperville, Illinois

PAT ARMSTRONG

Located in a typical suburban setting in Naperville, Illinois, Pat Armstrong models her garden after the native prairies that grew long before subdivisions ever existed. Since 1983 Pat has worked to make her one-third acre resemble the setting that our first pioneers encountered here. Pat's husband Chuck designed their passive solar home with a contemporary design that blends well with the colors and textures of a native midwestern landscape. Starting with a new home, Pat began her gardening with nothing. Today she has more than 240 species of plants, all native to the midwestern landscape.

A small creek borders the Armstrongs' property. When they first excavated the

Prairie rose (*Rosa setigera*) and arrowwood (*Viburnum dentatum*).

lawn, they designed a swale to help carry groundwater from the house. Thus, the back of the property and the house are set slightly higher than the middle of the property. This change in elevation gives a gentle rolling feeling to the yard and avoids the practice of strategically placed burms, which often have an artificial and deliberate effect. The midwestern landscape is flatter than other parts of the country, so creating a garden with slight rises and falls in the land offers pleasant surprises. Pat's technique of changing elevations to direct water runoff at a small creek has a more natural effect than simply making little mounds around the property. She has incorporated gentle

Left: Pat Armstrong's native prairie plants include switchgrass; black-eyed Susan; prairie coneflower; downy sunflower; stiff sunflower; beebalm; purple coneflower; purple prairie clover; June grass; rosinweed; bicknell sedge; yellow coneflower; rattlesnake master; wild quinine; and aromatic sumac.

Goldenrod *(Solidago altissima)* and New England aster *(Aster novae-angliae)*. Photo by Pat Armstrong.

movement into the entire landscape, which contributes to the feeling of space, since the eye travels slowly around the property rather than in one quick sweep. In addition, Pat's design has three separate types of prairie arranged along the different contours of the garden. By dividing her prairie into three sections that blend together gracefully and yet are as distinct as any layers in a garden border, Pat has achieved a marvelous aesthetic balance.

First, near the house and at the bottom of the swale, the seeded shortgrass prairie is predominately buffalo grass, *Buchloe dactyloides*, a shortgrass prevalent in Kansas and Nebraska. This area is Pat's lawn, yet it is also thick with prairie flowers or forbs like Prairie Clover, which were seeded by the runoff from the other areas on the way to the creek. Nevertheless, the area has a shorter appearance with a fine texture that opens and leads your eye outward to the next area, a middle-grass prairie.

In this section Pat has prairie dropseed, side-oats grama, and little bluestem as main grasses, and the forbes include baptisia, butterfly weed, purple coneflower, coreopsis, prairie phlox, and many less common species. Near the back of their property and slightly higher, she has plants typical of a tall-grass prairie. Here she has Indian grass, compass plant, rattlesnake master, switchgrass, and big blue stem. She also has a clump of staghorn sumac at the edge of the property. As Pat points out, a flat, green lawn does nothing to enhance your view. However, Pat's prairie is so captivating that you really don't see other houses, and the sweep of the prairie tends to carry your eye through the short-, middle-, and tall-grass prairies to the sky. Pat explains, "The idea was, as I looked out of my house, my eye would go up the lawn, up the middlegrass, over the tall-grass and would be carried into the sky."

In addition to herbaceous prairie plants, Pat has five species of sumac, which are a genus of native trees and shrubs that tend to grow by suckers spreading out from the edge to form a wide mound effect. Besides the staghorn sumac at the border, she uses the cutleaf sumac, a finer-textured plant next to the house. The lowest growing sumac, the fragrant sumac, serves as a foundation planting near the shorter area of the prairie grasses. As well as the graceful form of the sumac, Pat keeps the native trees like cottonwoods and hawthorns if they sprout in her garden.

As a canopy for many native woodland wildflowers and small native shrubs, Pat has a mature sixty-foot burr oak in the front of her house that creates a site for a burst of bloom in April and May. Since the soil in a twenty- to thirty-foot radius around the tree was not disturbed during construction of the house, and four inches of wood chips were added to cover the weedy brome grass, the oak survived. Under it Pat planted over a hundred species of woodland shrubs, ferns, and wildflowers. Her determination to save the large oak tree required her to protect the entire area under the canopy of the tree. (Oaks are particularly specific in their growing requirements; they must not have their root systems disturbed if they are to survive.) Because Pat knows how these native plants grow in the wild, she can have the range of prairie and woodland habitats that were common in the Midwest many years ago.

Another oak species that thrives in the limestone soils of the region is the Chinquapin oak. Pat started her own from seed. Although many oak species available in the nursery trade are not well suited for the high pH soils found throughout much of the Midwest, the Chinquapin is a

Purple prairie clover (*Petalostemon purpureum*); rattlesnake master (*Eryngium yuccifolium*); and rosinweed (*Silphium integrifolium*).

native that deserves wider recognition and should become more widely available.

Other woody flowering plants Pat grows include roses, but Pat's are all native and do not have the mildews, blackspot, and aphids so commonly associated with most commercial roses. One very large bush is the Illinois rose (*Rosa setigera*), which blooms later than the other species, sometimes growing as tall as five or six feet and equally broad. The two species of prairie roses that Pat has can be distinguished by their foliage—one has bluish leaves, the other has a shinier cast. Otherwise, they are difficult to distinguish. All of these native roses have a single row of petals and pink flowers from May through June. Still they are very hardy and have bright red-orange fruit in late summer and fall, so their appeal lasts through the seasons. Thus, as you walk around Pat's garden you do experience the expanses of grass mixed with flowers, but the prairie plants connect to the plants found at the borders of prairies and to those native to the woodlands.

Except for the area under their large burr oak, the Armstrongs' land was regraded during the construction of their house. Initially, Pat planned to sow the prairie seeds in the late spring or early summer. However, as often happens, they moved into their new house five months behind schedule and she had to plant the seeds in late October. This meant planting the prairie at a very inopportune time. But she had the bags of prairie seed and decided it was more important to start her garden than to wait and possibly regrade the property after a winter of uncovered, weather-washed soil. As a result, some of the initial seeding did not take. Pat adds now with a smile, "You wouldn't believe it, but the first year this was solid Queen

Royal catchfly (*Silene regia*) and purple prairie clover (*Petalostemon purpureum*).

Anne's lace and red clover. I just mowed it off and when I found a prairie plant, I would mark it and weed around it, so it would get sun. And they just came; they just kept coming and coming."

She also planted transplants of prairie grasses and flowers that she had grown from seed herself or bought from local nurseries. Thus, in part of her garden the plants came primarily from seeds, and in that area the plants are smaller and more interspersed. In other areas they are primarily from transplants, and there the plants are larger and grow in clumps. Even though the areas started with

seedlings, and seeds use the same species, the final effect is quite distinct. The area grown from seeds is a light, fine-textured blend of color and form, while the area planted with transplants has various masses of color and heights. However, because they are native prairie plants, they share their uniqueness; neither area settles for the clipped yews and pink petunias so prevalent just beyond the Armstrong property line.

Pat was delighted to discover native plants that she did not plant appearing in her garden, either from seed carried in and deposited throughout the swale when it rained, or perhaps from within the soil itself and uncovered during the grading of the land. Although she does weed out the nonnative plants, she enjoys discovering new native additions from time to time. Pat's detailed knowledge of the plants of the region and of natural history in general enables her to manage her garden successfully.

As a matter of fact, people who are restoring a native prairie use only seeds that are collected within a fifty-mile radius of the prairie being restored, to ensure that the plants will be as genetically close as possible to the original prairie plants that existed in that region. With such local genotypes, the restored prairie is very similar if not identical to the prairies growing in that location for thousands of years. These prairies become museums, laboratories, and havens for endangered groups of plants.

Pat feels the seed source must reflect the use and purpose of the garden. Although she uses local seed sources as much as possible in her garden, when she began the quantities of seed she needed were not available locally so she bought seed collected as far away as Central Illinois. Pat wanted to garden with native plants for pleasure as well as restoration, but the use of only local geno-types became a secondary concern. Pat agrees we need places where local ecotypes are saved and promoted, but currently there are not enough sources for people to buy locally grown seeds. Gardeners are looking at native midwestern plants for gardens that are not just hardy and vigorous but also more ecologically sound and that have the grace and beauty reflecting a simpler, less cultivated time.

Since Pat found that beginning a native, naturalistic landscape is initially very labor-intensive, she recommends starting small, especially if you are a beginner. Pat spent hours tending her garden for the first year. Thus, unless the new garden is like her own, a new home site, she suggests starting small and adding to it each year. Now Pat considers her maintenance minimal, but when she began, she had to be able to recognize many different species of native plants and Eurasian weeds in order to have only the de-

Snowing on the prairie.

sired plants remain. (When she spots a tall grass like Indian grass growing in the shortgrass area, she digs it out and moves it.) Now, however, other than always keeping an eye out for intruders, Pat's primary maintenance responsibility is her annual fire.

Pat burns her prairie garden in the spring because, as she puts it, "in the winter it looks pretty." Although Pat lives inside the village limits and open fires are normally prohibited, she gets a special permit because fire is the traditional method of controlling nonnative weeds in prairies as well as tree and shrub species. Prairie fires rolled along the flat expanses of rich grassland for thousands of years, helping to keep those perennial plants whose roots were not touched by the fire and that came back as vigorously as if they had received a good pruning. Thus, Pat says she burns her prairie "because a prairie needs burning since the fire kills weed seeds but not prairie plants." She adds, "Naperville is a very forward-thinking community." Pat believes that by permitting her annual burning, her community reinforces its commitment to its own environmental future.

Pat contends that burning the prairie is less toxic than applying chemicals needed to grow many nonnative plants successfully. She tells her neighbors when she is going to

Prairie burn in late March.

burn, and she asks friends and students to help by standing near the trees she wants to save and putting out the fire if it comes too close. The fire goes out by itself when it reaches the end of the prairie area or comes to a sidewalk or into green lawn grass. Pat notes, "Green grass doesn't burn very well; it smokes and smolders but then goes out." The first year Pat burned she did not have very much to burn, but each year as her prairie becomes more established the annual process becomes larger and, as Pat puts it, "more spectacular." She remembers one rather less than enthusiastic neighbor's response to Pat's announcement of her burn by saying, "Good, what's going to come up next?" When she said "Oh, it will come back better than ever," he just said, "Oh." However, regardless of the few people in Pat's area who are bound by more traditional ideas of clipped bluegrass lawns and trimmed evergreen hedges, Pat's community recognizes her collection as the carefully tended cultivated plants they are.

As Pat walks through her garden she points out the compass plants, rosinweed, the wild quinine, and the showy goldenrod whose beauty she notes as certainly as any gardener boasting prized roses or chrysanthemums. One interesting aspect of Pat's selection of plants is her choice of plants native to this region that grow in limestone soils. Also, she grows plants with red foliage in the fall and lots of purple flowers, because she happens to like purple. In fact, Pat's garden proves that combining purple and orange doesn't have to be tricky.

Along with the many shades of lavender, Pat has the lovely clear orange of the butterfly weed, and the yellows of the prairie coneflower, compass plant, and coreopsis. She notes that the combination of purple prairie clover and orange butterfly weed is a perfect example of how to use both orange and lavender successfully and naturally. In the prairie, orange is not only natural, but it adds warmth and the sense of vibrant electricity flowing through the hot summer landscape. The stately, tall *Aster novae-angliae* or New England aster, which grows well in the alkaline soils of the region, dominates the autumn landscape. It gives an effect somewhat similar to chrysanthemums only much taller, stretching four to five feet, and hardier. As Pat points out, it is "so beautiful in the fall, I've just put it all around the area." Some of her other autumn favorites are the tall prairie grasses, stiff goldenrod, aromatic aster, and smooth blue aster. She adds, "I've tried everything that grows in prairies, and some things just don't make it." Thus, she has found that the plants that grow in higher pH soil do well, but those that prefer sandy or acidic soil don't grow well. The plants that do well are those typical of a tall-grass prairie and the vegetation that covered much of this region of the Midwest centuries ago, long before the lawn mower was even dreamed of.

Culver's root (*Veronicastrum virginicum*); oxeye sunflower (*Heliopsis helianthoides*); and switchgrass (*Panicum virgatum*).

Pat now works as a teacher and consultant to people who want to start natural gardens like her own. In this way she hopes to really restore the tall-grass prairie to the Midwest and benefit the environment by eliminating pesticides and tools such as lawn mowers, which intensify some of the problems of modern suburban life, including chemical and noise pollution. With her own prairie garden as an example, she demonstrates how to have a garden that reduces our sense of hectic cities and draws us into the natural world around us.

By establishing this unique style of gardening, Pat has helped her neighbors understand how a prairie grows.

Butterfly weed (*Asclepias tuberosa*); big bluestem (*Andropogon gerardi*); and rosinweed (*Silphium integrifolium*).

Left: Bergamot (*Monarda fistulosa*); daisy fleabane (*Erigeron annuus*); and prairie dock (*Silphium terebinthinaceum*).

- *To help large native oaks survive the construction of a new house, cord off the entire area under the drip line of the tree and do not disturb it. A native wildflower garden easily flourishes in soil under a mature native tree enriched with four inches of wood-chip mulch.*

- *Shrub roses indigenous to the region grow easily without an intensive regime of sprays and fertilizers. The hips of native roses left on the plants to mature accent the late-summer, fall, and winter garden beautifully.*

- *Learn to identify the seedlings as well as mature plants of cultivated and weed species.*

- *Try to use locally collected seeds of native specimens to help maintain the genetic integrity of the species variety.*

- *Begin your garden on a small scale and gradually increase its size.*

- *To remove many nonnative weeds, burn a prairie garden early in the spring.*

At first, Pat's neighbors called the village office to complain about weeds adjoining their property. (Naperville has a lawn ordinance that states the home owner must keep lawns cut to six inches.) But Pat did keep what lawn she had cut to six inches. However, since the ordinance does not require people to cut off cultivated plants to a height of six inches, when the inspectors came out to look at her "weeds," she pointed out and classified the prairie plants and wildflowers she was growing as cultivated plants. The weed or lawn ordinance did not apply. As a result, Pat's garden has flourished and served as an example for others who want to grow a more natural, native landscape.

Take a look at the photographs on these pages. Prairie gardening is on the rise!

Monticello, Iowa

JIM AND JOY ADAMS

Near Iowa's east central region are woodlands filled with wildflowers and open spaces with sweeping flower beds. In this wooded site overlooking a ravine, Jim and Joy Adams garden. The native cedars, oaks, and hornbeams, the cherries and apples all provide shelter and background for the garden from one season to the next. As Joy remarks, "You can just walk around, and you can't help enjoying the beauty no matter what season it is. I travel and see beauty, and then I realize that it is right here around us if we open our eyes." The grace of their garden design, as it flows from the woodland to the open spaces, makes the visitor yearn for instruction in the Adams method.

Jim and Joy do have much to teach the mid-western gardener. For instance, many people consider the native cedar, *Thuja occidentalis*, a weedy tree and replace it with Colorado blue spruce or arborvitae, but the older trees add a soft texture and easy movement to the garden. Jim considers cedars one of the best evergreens for the Midwest. They are resistant to the needle blight that affects the spruces. Unlike the arborvitae, they are drought tolerant. When piled with snow that hangs over their tops, they turn the garden into a fairyland. Although grown for beauty and dependability, cedars supply birds' food as well. Joy smiles when she says, "There are thirty-three species of birds that like them."

Another native considered a weed by

At the edge of the woods the annual impatiens, ageratum, amaranthus, celosia, marigolds, and nicotiana blend with the flowering purple coneflowers *(Echinacea purpurea)* and *Lythrum* 'Morden Gleam'.

Left: Purple coneflower *(Echinacea purpurea); Lythrum* 'Morden's Gleam'; amaranthus; ageratum; and summer balsam, highlighted by marigolds and daylilies.

some is the staghorn sumac *(Rhus typhina)*, which proves to be a full backdrop for blooming plants. When its leaves turn bright red in the fall, it offers a vivid display of its own.

Of course, a garden that features trees must overcome shade. Only careful planning enables this garden to soak up the patches of full sun as it moves through the sky. Ferns, woodland wildflowers, hostas, and spring-flowering bulbs fill in the areas of deeper shade.

Although light shade prevents plants from drying out rapidly, plants under trees tend to get tall and lanky and then fall over. Reducing fertilizer slows the growth, but due to the lower light some stretch results regardless of the amount of fertilizer they use. For this reason Jim designs

Snow covers the native cedars.

each flower bed to catch the sun as it moves through the garden, planning each group of plants so they receive the maximum amount of light. In the spring near the trees, plants come out more slowly than they do in more exposed gardens nearby. The bordering trees help protect the garden from any late-spring or early-fall frosts. A site protected by many surrounding trees reduces damage done by the rapid swing in temperature so characteristic of the midwestern climate. In this way the moderating effect of the trees outweighs the lack of light.

In a garden featuring trees, vines like *Parthenocissus quinefolia* (Virginia creeper) and *Celastrus scandens* (American bittersweet) climb to provide color and textural interest. Even poison ivy winding into the trees during the fall turns a brilliant red and is enjoyed at a distance! During the summer, *Clematis* sp. wind flower-laden tendrils up the trunks of trees. Since they usually freeze to the ground, they produce only a dwarf version of the show seen in milder climates. Even though the trees do shade the roots of the *Clematis* during the hot Iowa summers, they develop slowly. Typically seven years of growth pass before a really stunning display appears.

Although rich clay loam soils are typically synonymous with many regions of the Midwest, areas of different soils, such as this sandy loam soil, result from the glaciation that covered the Midwest several times during prehistoric times. The soil in this garden began forming about 440 million years ago during the Silurian glaciation. The character of the soil itself is a very fine sand, called "blow sand," deposited by the air. The rolling topography and the less fertile sandy forest soil make the Adamses' land less valuable for farming but excellent for growing many perennial plants. The use of raised beds to promote rapid drainage in more clay-laden soils becomes unnecessary when the sandy soils and rolling hills drain rapidly. The rolling characteristics of the land make for excellent gardens.

The other crucial factor of midwestern soil is the pH or degree of acidity and alkalinity. Like most of the Midwest, the soil is not acidic enough for azaleas and rhododendrons. If they are to thrive, these ericaceous plants need soil amendments to lower the pH to a more acidic level. With doses of special acidifying fertilizers or sulfur compounds like ammonium sulfate, the pH can be adjusted well enough.

Roses do not need an adjustment in pH, but Jim and Joy do give them special handling. The soil in this region is a rich, sandy loam, but organic matter like peat moss improves the soil. Even though the soil drains rapidly and

Hollyhocks *(Alcea rosea)*; love-lies-bleeding *(Amaranthus caudatus)*; salvia; and purple coneflower *(Echinacea purpurea)*. Photo by Pam Wolfe.

the plant roots do not sit in heavy, poorly draining clay soils, organic matter improves the texture and facilitates nutrient uptake. Sweet alyssum planted as an annual ground cover under the roses helps hold down weeds; reflects light, which cools the soil; and prevents the wind from desiccating the soil around the plants. These bright white annuals serve the function of a summer mulch.

The Dubuque Arboretum inspired the rose garden. Jim says, "I didn't know you could grow roses that well in the Midwest, and when I saw those, I kept in the back of my mind that I had to have a rose garden." Strong examples like the Dubuque Arboretum help instruct and inspire gardeners. Many roses don't mind the midwestern heat if they are watered regularly. To avoid getting water on the leaves, particularly in the most humid season, Jim uses a trickle hose. This reduces foliar leaf fungus diseases like black spot. But he adds, "Even overhead watering is better than allowing them to get too dry."

In general, watering remains the garden's prime maintenance requirement. Without a soaking rain each week, watering by hand is important. For plants that wilt in the heat of the summer and plants that must not dry out, Jim uses a drip irrigation system. A soaker hose helps plants that are particularly susceptible to heat and drought stress. In addition to roses, *Dicentra spectabilis* (bleeding heart) and *Astilbe* need plenty of moisture for them to hold their foliage during the summer.

Preparing the beds for winter demands rigorous attention. In late fall or early winter a foot of sandy, loam soil covers the roses. The soil gets layered with leaves or straw for additional insulation. He removes these in the spring before the plants show signs of new growth. Of the over two hundred roses, they usually lose only one or two. Their technique is simple and effective and much more attractive than rose cones.

Successive flowering combinations bloom from early spring to late fall. Even in the azalea beds Joy adds perennials and annuals to blend with the shrubs and to carry the bloom of spring into the summer. With the white of 'Northern Lights' azaleas, clear medium blue of perennial salvia, and pale sky blue of *Campanula*, the clear red tulips 'Paul Richter' create an explosion of early color. Another favorite spring combination includes the various species of *Pulmonaria*

Hosta with dame's rocket (*Hesperis matronalis*) in early spring.

(lungwort) and *Mertensia* (Virginia bluebells) to which Joy adds dwarf irises. A few weeks later bearded irises and poppies take over. A light peach poppy blooms next to a white iris that has a blue edge on the tip of each petal.

In the woodlands of late spring, wildflowers like the wild campanula and bluebell are, as Joy notes, "quite spectacular." Later the hillside becomes a blanket of lavender when the dame's rocket *(Hesperis matronalis)* blooms. By late summer another native, purple coneflower *(Echinacea purpurea)* blooms with such brilliance Jim finds he gets anxious to see what's going to happen next. Some flowering displays are so breathtaking that it seems they can never be equaled. Yet a new season brings new splendor. Scattering seeds of wildflowers like Virginia bluebells *(Mertensia virginica)* on the top of the hill eventually brings the whole hillside into bloom at once. Naturalizing different flowers at different times of year comes from experience.

Some species "travel" around the gardens. Self-sowing plants like the love-lies-bleeding *(Amaranthus caudatus)* flower with purple coneflower, pink *Monarda didyma,* and the pink *Phlox* in tall waves of pinks and lavenders. Even when the effect is showy, a good balance will not last long. If the coneflowers are not weeded out, they will not allow the phlox to survive. In other spots the phlox must be weeded

to allow the coneflowers to grow. Vigorous plants eventually choke out other species, destroying the balance of the planting. Even in natural areas some balancing of aggressive plants takes work.

Bleeding heart *(Dicentra spectabilis).*

Of course, Jim and Joy add new plants to their already varied collection. Recent favorites include hardy pansies or violas that they started from seed through a mail-order catalog. These new plants bloomed continually all summer even when the old flowers were not removed. Besides the *Viola cornuta, Ligularia* 'Marjory Fisk' blends well with *Ranunculus* and *Phlox.* Although vigorous *Heliop-*

sis often crowds out less vigorous plants, natives like *Anemone* and *Asclepias* (butterfly weed) are not at all aggressive.

Jim and Joy are often pleasantly surprised with a plant combination that grows from self-sown seed, but most of their garden results from careful planning and experience. As Joy explains, "We like to choreograph the colors with different combinations. You know, I don't have a favorite color, and I can't say I have a favorite flower. In some beds we start with blue, in another area pink. A lot of people don't like orange, but orange and blue complement each other well, as do violet and yellow." After the initial color, they add others to complete the ensemble. Perennial purple salvia, orange daylily, and the soft yellow of the daylily 'Hudson Valley' give a pleasing effect. Joy points out that in nature all color combinations work together.

Joy advises, "The best way to plant for succession is to take notes through the year. This assures that the cultivars put together really blend and complement each other. Write down what works and what doesn't. Keep a garden diary, even a sketchy one. In addition to color, combinations of foliage add depth to the garden. It's fun to play with textures and colors. The leaves are important. So many people just put all the same textures of leaves together. Using annuals helps to tie the beds together as well as link the different seasons. You can't put all of your spring here and your fall there. You've got to put a clump of spring, a clump of spring, a clump of spring. We started the gardens that way. We have a clump of spring, a clump of summer, and a clump of fall near each other. We repeat this pattern in all the beds. Then we fill in.

Daffodils; tulips; and bleeding heart in the early spring.

This way you get the breath of the flowers throughout, and in the distance it all blends together as one garden." Preparing consecutive displays enables the garden to peak repeatedly throughout the year.

Clumps of *Pulmonaria* and iris combine throughout the garden for their spring planting. Later light peach poppy and white irises edged in light blue flower together throughout the garden. The later summer bouquet of purple coneflowers complements the lilies. After being cut back, the free-flowering digitalis 'Gold Spears' blooms again. Some biennials like the foxglove spread by seeds that can be transplanted to other areas after sprouting. For highlights late in the afternoon of early spring and late fall as well as summer evenings, whites scattered throughout the garden show up like beacons. In addition to some white azaleas and white and blue irises, white and yellow tiny flowers on tall stalks of the wildflower daisy fleabane mix throughout the beds later in the summer. Joy says, "It adds kind of a baby's breath effect to the garden." Taking it out after it blooms keeps it from becoming weedy.

Also, for the fall, *Solidaster,* a cross between goldenrod and an aster, gives a bright, warm glow to the garden. Although no particular combination lasts too long, Jim and Joy are too busy anticipating the next show to regret the end of the last one. "You're sad because the spring flowers are gone, but up come the irises," Joy says. "When they're fading here come the peonies. When the daylilies are fading, there's a consolation—up come the dahlias."

- *If your yard is shady, place your beds carefully to catch the maximum amount of sunlight.*
- *If you surround your garden with some trees, you will reduce the damage from late and early frosts, which usually hit open gardens more severely.*
- *Roses need ample water. Don't let them suffer water stress.*
- *Water roses with a trickle hose to slow the spread of water-borne diseases.*
- *A ground cover of white annual alyssum around roses helps reflect some of the intense summer heat so deleterious to roses.*
- *To protect roses during the winter, layer a foot of soil on the plants and then top that with straw or leaves.*
- *Self-sowing annuals add variety to perennials.*
- *Combining colors, as in a large Dutch Master bouquet, produces gardens that look like flower arrangements.*
- *Keep a garden diary—even a sketchy one.*
- *White flowers and foliage light up the garden in the early evening.*
- *The native wildflower daisy fleabane adds the texture and color of baby's breath to the garden.*
- *Changing the annuals used each year with the perennials creates a whole new look for the garden.*

As the summer progresses, dahlias, staked in the foreground, will grow above the spiderflower (*Cleome*), celosia, marigold, ageratum, and polyanthus roses. Daylilies, delphiniums, and impatiens flower in the background.

The annuals that tie the beds together may stay the same each year like the bed of impatiens that covers the ground under a sweep of salmon, cream, and light yellow Asiatic lilies or the alyssum under the roses. They may change each year—white begonias and coleus one year, pink petunias and *Nicotiana* the next. This gives the whole garden a new look. A small change shifts the accent from one color to another. One year Jim put marigolds with hostas. Then coleus and white begonias accented the garden; another year caladium; the next, white *Nicotiana* with *Calendula*, zinnias, and petunias.

Gardens like Joy and Jim's attest to the way colors are the artistic extension of the gardener. One of Joy's favorite combinations—purple mullein *(Verbascum phoeniceum)* and *Lychnis viscaria* 'splendens Flore Pleno'—flowers while the irises and *Pulmonaria* finish blooming. *Pulmonaria* are a spring favorite. Since *Pulmonaria* self-sow, naturalizing them at the edge of the woodland easily fills out the planting. The *Pulmonaria* 'Sissinghurst White' lights up with white flowers and silver on its leaves. Although *Pulmonaria* look like the wild bluebells, their foliage stays all through the growing season, making them a favorite ground cover when not in flower.

In late spring, *Coreopsis*, *Gaillardia*, and shasta daisy fill out the beds. In the late summer, asters, both native and newer, showier cultivars, take their place. With them the small orange- and yellow-flowered candy lily *(Belamcanda)* blooms into August. One interesting combination that sounds unusual but is very deliberate uses orange tiger lilies and pink *Astilbe*. Tall pink *Amaranthus* blends into this pink and orange combination with the style and grace of a large Dutch Master bouquet. The garden looks at once, sophisticated and inviting.

Joy and Jim find the time caring for their garden is not really work. As Joy says, "We don't spend a lot of time watching television or going to movies. We enjoy the time in the garden and find it is a good way to enjoy the beauty around us." Today finds many people passively absorbing the world. But by working with their surroundings, the Adamses interact with their environment and are stewards for its future.

Chicago, Illinois
CHUCK HARRIS

When Chuck Harris started his garden in the heart of Chicago nearly nine years ago, his neighborhood was crowded, run-down, and neglected. Today signs of a regenerating spirit abound, and the advantages of living and gardening in an urban area are apparent in the vibrant but peaceful garden that borders his old frame house.

When Chuck bought the house he was attracted to the available side lot, as well as amenities that include being able to walk to work, living in the heart of the cultural center of a major city, and enjoying a climate moderated, if only by a few degrees, by Lake Michigan.

Chuck began the garden renewal before the house was renovated. Doing all the work himself, he labored on the garden four years before he moved into the house. When the rebuilding became a long-term personal commitment, a degree of acceptance and appreciation developed among his neighbors. "When I bought

it, it was incredible how inexpensive it was. I was the first new entry into the neighborhood. It was pretty wild, pretty tough back then, and now I couldn't buy here because the value has gone up so much. Other people

Daffodils with the weeping cherry.

who also are gardeners moved into the neighborhood. It's worked out fine—a great climate and a great location. The fact that I did all the work myself had a positive influence on the situation. People tended to respect what I did."

As the first newcomer to this Chicago inner-city neighborhood, Chuck was mindful of security and privacy. The enclosed garden has become a natural way to benefit internally from a place that contrasts with all that surrounds it, to live a somewhat protected life in the densely populated, external city.

Trellises soften the garden's walls and tie the design together with repeating vines, creating a certain visual rhythm throughout the garden. An oasis of intimacy emerges in the midst of the urban landscape. Climbing hydrangea that receives only a few hours of light in the morning grows contentedly on one trellis in the front garden. A mixture of trumpet vine, clematis, yellow climbing roses,

Left: The rose 'Scarlet Meidiland'; variegated ribbon grass *(Phalaris arundinacea* 'Lutea picta'); and *Artemisia.*

the early-summer-blooming Kentucky wisteria (*Wisteria macrostachya*), and the fall eruption of the late-summer flowers of the silver lace vine form a thick mat on the fence along the front walk. Although canes of the climbing rose 'Golden Shower' die back during the winter, their summer growth restores the long eight-foot stretches by midsummer. The clematis climbs the trellis niche of the garage, filling the gray background with a clear blue and adding space, height, and color to the garden. Two trellises on the side of the garage are recessed in the siding to give them the appearance of niches framing the clematis.

The evolution of Chuck's property began with a redesign of the Chicago boxcar–style house, where one room leads to the next. By purchasing the side lot, Chuck could swing the main entry around to the side and allow the front walk to wind through the side lot, as through a spacious courtyard. Since the ground is often wet during the winter and spring, a boardwalk walkway adds warmth to the plant material and lifts the walk a few inches above the garden. The house is now an open airy space composed of living areas and light, and the garden is an enclosed space with separate yet connected areas that have become an outdoor extension of the living environment. (The flexibility to change the whole plan makes the house and garden an unusual blend of old and new.) Changing the topography to make the sunken garden and above-grade walkway adds space in the vertical plane. Winding through the center of the garden, a mulch path becomes narrower as the garden grows wider, replacing the strip of worn lawn.

Spiraea japonica 'Little Princess'; *Miscanthus sinensis* var. *gracillimus*; *Coreopsis lanceolata*; and *Lilium* 'Enchantment'.

The dining area opens onto a terrace shaded by a pergola that is covered with a grapevine on the south side and the pink Hal's honeysuckle on the north side. A concrete patio joins the design yet remains functional and durable. Chuck recalls, "I debated whether I should use wood or not, and then I realized being on grade level, concrete would make sense." This terrace actually displays warmth, a quality usually missing with concrete. A simple decorative design drawn into the concrete during construction softens the material and directs the eye to the center.

The overall design of the garden repeats the circular pattern of the nearby fish pond. The pool is a large, sunken, seven-foot-wide galvanized tub, a livestock watering tank now dug into the ground. Since the bottom is painted black, it appears to be deeper than its two feet. Its sides become overgrown with plants each summer, hiding the uniform edge of the trough. With a decorative circulating pump Chuck purchased from a local pet store and goldfish eating the insect larvae, the water remains clear as it contributes a welcome sound to the garden. Near the pond, clumps of Siberian iris and the ornamental grass *Miscanthus sinensis* var. *gracillimus* give a flowing line to the circular form. The trellis, pond, walkway, and patio flow together in an enticing series of circular elements.

The tall *Miscanthus* grows thick and robust and prompts movement in the garden. The sound of wind moving through the grass can be as tranquil as the sound of water. The smells and sounds of the garden enhance this sense of enclosure. As Chuck puts it,

- *Vines growing over a trellis soften the landscape and take up little space in a city garden.*
- *A simple device like a sunken watering trough easily makes a small fish pond.*
- *In a small garden, gradual changes in elevation can create a sense of space.*
- *Rich soil is the most important factor in getting a plant to flourish.*
- *Plant for texture as well as bloom. Using vegetables as ornamentals provides a striking effect in the garden.*
- *Ornamental grasses lend the effect of sound to the garden, even through the late fall.*
- *Keep a garden journal to help plan for the future.*
- *Clean out diseased and dead leaves and flowers to cut down on the spread of diseases and the insects that spread them.*

Weigela florida 'Variegata'; hosta; Juniper sp.; weeping Yoshino cherry.

Seeds are economical and over the years yielded much of the garden's abundance. In March when Chuck's urge to garden becomes overwhelming, he enjoys starting plants indoors. However, they remain a frustrating effort, and Chuck winds up purchasing many plants from a nursery. Several plants were started by dividing plants that grew in his parents' home; irises from his parents' home came from his grandparents' home. Sedum divides easily this way and remains a favorite for dependability and summer flowers in sunny spots.

Keeping a journal of the garden provides valuable information regarding the best times for planting in this area. A record of when plants were planted and bloomed follows the progress of the garden and gives clues on making improvements for the next year. Chuck elaborates: "It's really a nice way to involve yourself with the progress of the yard. Sometimes I learn from mistakes as with *Agapanthus*, which I planted in early April and they froze to the ground twice before they got started. Next year I won't put them in quite so early."

Maintenance with water and chemicals is minimal. Supplemental water is only added to new plantings until they become established. The rest of the garden depends on natural rainfall. The heat of the midwestern summer is moderated by the lake, making the inner city an ideal area for gardening. In a very protected spot next to the patio, which receives only a few hours of morning sun, *Ligularia stenocephala* 'The Rocket' blooms with tall yellow candles.

Chicago, Illinois   69

Shaded from the intense noonday sun and standing in moist soil, *Ligularia* still wilts on hot days. Even adequate water will not keep plants acclimatized to cooler zones happy on a hot midwestern afternoon. But given careful placement, many unusual specimens will grow here. Cleaning and cutting out diseased plant material reduces the spread of infestations and the need for chemical application. Chuck emphasizes, "When my roses develop a blighted area, I cut it off. I'd rather mutilate the plant than deal with treating it." Rhododendrons and azaleas do get a regular application of acidifying fertilizer since the soil is not acidic enough to grow these plants.

Winter protection comes from a layer of leaves raked onto the beds from the yard. In the spring Chuck clears this away from the beds, leaving some in the back of the beds and putting the rest on the compost pile. By deteriorating in place, the leaves replenish nutrients used by the growing plants, although excess debris decays slowly and looks unsightly.

Chuck leaves garden cleanup until spring to allow time to enjoy the plant forms and colors during the winter. *Miscanthus* plumes stand like light golden flags against the winter light. The dark thistle-shaped seedpods of the coneflowers stand out against the golden tones, giving depth and dimension to the winter landscape.

Establishing a garden takes time and patience. Some people are perfecting a garden, trying to get it just "right" and then leave it exactly that way; this garden changes a little each year.

Once a garden approaches maturity, the number of hours needed drops off, but Chuck still finds he spends an hour after work in the summer just "putzing around in the garden." He admits he spends less time than when he began but notes, "Now rather than twelve hours a weekend, I usually don't spend more than four to six hours. It varies; there's more to do in the spring. I didn't really know how much time it would take, but I just got more and more drawn into it. It truly did evolve."

Left: Large leaves of rhubarb with red shrub rose.

portant part of the collection, but 'Betty Prior' remains the faithful performer with its simple, single flowers supplying the grace and aristocratic air expected of a fine rose. A clump of *Dictamnus* gas plant, well suited for a spot in a long-lived collection, fills out the back of the 'Betty Prior' Garden with its thick attractive foliage and solid mass of white flowers.

Nearby, borrowed from the inspiration of the great English gardener Gertrude Jekyll, a cloud of baby's breath draped with the vines of white sweet peas looks like Belgian lace draping the shrub roses or Asiatic lilies. Karen exclaims, "'Betty Prior' with baby's breath is fantastic!" Cut back after the first blooms fade, baby's breath blooms twice.

On long flower stalks from feathery foliage, the small flower clusters of garden heliotrope (*Valeriana officinalis*) bloom with a light, distinctive fragrance during July and August. The white blossoms, tinted a light shade of pink, hang like little clouds and set off many other plants with their spotlike quality. These two airy plants produce a fullness to the beds during mid-to-late summer. *Cimicifuga simplex* produces full, tight racemes of white blooms that at first glance could be confused with *Astilbe*

x *arendsii*. They bloom earlier than *C. racemosa*, the native species, and have shorter, less arching flowers. They lighten the late-summer shadows and cool the warm tones of *Helenium* with their clumps of white candles.

Later during the summer and fall, the garden lightens its texture and color with the cultivar of *Boltonia* 'Snowbank', which holds its shape and is a reliable, easily grown choice covered with masses of small daisy-

Floribunda rose 'Betty Prior'; baby's breath *(Gypsophila paniculata)*; and sweet peas. Photo by Pam Wolfe.

like flowers. *Boltonia* blends well with silvery lavender Russian sage (*Perovskia*) and clear blue fall asters, *Aster frikartii* 'Wonder of Staffa'. The autumn anemones in white or pink blend to a cool, delicate combination contrasting with the yellows and light browns of early fall.

During July, in an area of filtered light, the dissected gray foliage and

tiny lavender flowers of Russian sage mixed with the German strain of lupines, *Lupinus* 'White Popsicle', creates a lovely duet. These lupines perform, whereas the climate is too hot and the soil is usually too alkaline for the Russell hybrids to survive.

Finding variety for the later part of summer, with its hotter temperatures and drop in rainfall, challenges most every midwestern gardener. The rush of bloom that characterizes May and June slows to a languid, almost imperceptible progression. Monkshood, one lovely late-summer blue entry, provides gorgeous rich purple flowers and makes excellent cut bouquets. The dark azure blue of *Aconitum carmichaelii* belies the considerably poisonous chemicals the plant produces. Small children should not play in this garden, and vegetables are not mixed in the display. The one-inch flowers have petals formed like hoods or helmets arranged on a central stalk like delphiniums. The intense blue complements the strong yellow of *Rudbeckia* 'Goldsturm' in a location shaded from the hottest part of the day. The plants in general perform best in moist, cool soil. The combination of Monkshood with pale Japanese lilies brings a cool glow to a hot, humid afternoon.

Karen finds *Rudbeckia* 'Gold Drop'

superior to 'Goldsturm' since "you can leave it without dividing it for at least five years." After two years the clump of 'Gold Drop' still remains as a small circle, whereas 'Goldsturm' spreads by aggressive rhizomes.

Warm tones are difficult to work with, particularly with Karen's predominately cool combinations, but one area of the garden features the

Sundrops *(Oenothera missourensis)* and baby's breath *(Gypsophila paniculata)*.

warm shades. Granted, even cool, pale yellows are easier to use than very intense colors, but the orange butterfly weed *(Asclepias tuberosa)* stands out as an exception. Butterfly weed has a clarity that goes with almost everything. In some areas get-

ting it established presents a challenge, as it favors well-drained soil, but once butterfly weed starts to grow, it shows itself to be a true native.

In general, Karen uses orange where it can show through some distant plant as a backlight. Bright yellow *Helianthus* grows behind the bed of asparagus and becomes a backdrop for the lacy foliage at the end of the garden. It carries the dissected color across the garden.

Perched on tall gladiolalike foliage, the small, spotted, warm-toned flowers of blackberry lily *(Belamcanda chinensis)* usually get lost in surrounding flowers. But Karen plants them in masses of at least three feet in diameter, and the small flowers seem to float together on top of the long stems, hovering like butterflies in the hot afternoon. Little pieces of blackberry lily will never produce this effect; large clumps are needed. In the fall these same slender stems, topped with clusters of blackberry-looking seeds, further warrant adding this plant to any midwestern garden.

A wide range of phlox fill the garden, from the creeping forms of May and June to the giants of August. All are subject to powdery mildew in the humid, late summer, but this rarely destroys the plant. Plants with some direct sunlight and good air movement stay freer of diseases. The ice-cream clumps of *Phlox carolina* 'Miss Lingard' bloom in June and July and

- *Arranging colors, forms, and textures with an eye to balance and rhythm keeps the garden from looking haphazard.*

- *When a plant is not in flower, the color and texture of the foliage should complement the setting.*

- *Since early-winter and spring frosts kill many shallow-rooted plants in heavy clay soils, mix one-third sand and one-third organic material with one-third soil to a depth of thirty inches in the planting bed.*

- *After plants have flowered, cut back perennials such as perennial flax* (Linum perenne) *to stimulate a second flush of flowers.*

- *Regularly add a light organic mulch like sawdust to make weeding easy; it decomposes quickly. The regular addition of a nitrogen fertilizer keeps the decaying organic matter from robbing nutrients from the garden.*

- *As plants come in and out of bloom, the focal point and pattern of color gradually shift throughout the season. Planning this evolution gives the garden the look of a perpetual bouquet.*

blend in size and texture with the light lemon shades of daylilies *(Hemerocallis)*. The creeping phlox 'Millstream Jupiter' gives a thick carpet of blue during May and June and grows next to *Veronica spicata* 'Blue Nana', which blooms heavily with light yellow-green foliage. Karen and Bill use many phlox cultivars, but during the spring this combination of blues blooms for over a month, and the yellow-green foliage complements and accentuates the cool flowers.

For those at a loss trying to plan plant combinations, Karen points out, "People get very frustrated trying to figure out how to put it together." She and Bill strive to demonstrate that a midwestern garden amounts to much more than a collection of plants that can survive the climate. Rather, it can become an extensive and exciting array of fantastic ensembles and gorgeous combinations. Karen and Bill's arrangements fit so naturally in the landscape that they appear obvious. Although the beds winding around their Iowa home bloom with seemingly effortless grace, these two energetic artists have poured skill and planning into every magnificent flower.

Delphinium x *belladonna* and *Clematis recta*.

An early-spring border highlights *Ajuga*; white bleeding heart (*Dicentra spectabilis* 'Alba'); *Narcissus* 'Geranium'; and 'China Pink' lily–flowered tulips and alliums—with the later daylily collection beginning to fill in. Photo by Emily Daniels.

as tight, attractive foliage habit. Picking a favorite among the many available is like choosing a favorite among a classroom of children. Together they produce color over broad sweeps of the garden. The old image of daylilies growing wild through a bed, overrunning everything, remains a myth believed only by those who are unaware of the breeding advances over the last twenty years. These showy performers, with the shrubs and ground covers, become the backbone of the garden. The daylilies start blooming in May with early bloomers like *Hemerocallis dumortieri*, a pale golden orange with thin grassy leaves, and continue into August with fine new tetraploid cultivars such as 'Fall Farewell'.

While using new cultivars of the old standards, the garden continually hosts new plants, expanding the scope and creating interest. One plant usually not seen produces a striking effect; *Crambe cordifolia* develops enormous two-foot, heart-shaped leaves and sprouts a six-foot-high cloud of tall, loose, tiny white flowers. The large wrinkly leaves give a lush jungle look to the border. Although previously considered to be limited only to zone six, it survives zone five's

temperature minimum of minus twenty degrees Fahrenheit.

Selecting new as well as dependable old cultivars arranged in a pleasing overall design makes the garden truly noteworthy. From old favorites near the untamed sections of the garden, like *Monarda* and *Cleome*, to stately selections such as the recent white cultivar of purple coneflower, *Echinacea purpurea* 'White Swan', and the mildew-resistant *Phlox carolina*, the progression of color through the beds unifies the design and ties the garden together. During the seasons, colors move through each bed and create a rhythm of movement for the eye to follow.

The clear red of the *Weigela* sets off the bright blue Siberian iris as the deep blue of the false indigo, *Baptisia*, glows next to the large single blossoms of the rosy red tree peony. As it finishes flowering, the pure white foxglove, a cultivar of *Digitalis purpurea*, highlights the late spring display. The pale, delicate yellows of 'Moonbeam' coreopsis and *Oenothera fruticosa youngii* replace the early spring blues complementing the Veronica varieties and *Lythrum* 'Morden Pink', as the garden's blue shades give way to a soft blend of pinks and yellow for the mid-

Feaverfew or matricaria (*Chrysanthemum parthenium*) masks peony foliage in front of the noninvasive purple loosestrife (*Lythrum* 'Morden Pink'), and smooth hydrangea (*Hydrangea arborescens* 'Annabelle') blooms in an island bed near the pond.

summer show. An excellent long-blooming performer, red valerian (*Centranthus ruber*) maintains glowing pink clusters throughout the beds from June to September.

In sunny spots the sedums and annuals give the garden mums and *Aster frikartii* a robust setting. Under the cool shade of the Amur cork tree a collection of softly tinted, elegant Japanese anemones tempers the sharp shadows of the shortening autumn days. Even before they bloom, their small rounded leaves, hanging from long slender stems, flutter in the breeze for a cooling movement. Although the heavy summer heat inhibits the late-summer thalictrums, so thoroughly enjoyed further north, at the edge of the wooded areas the meadow rue (*Thalictrum aquilegiafolium*) supplies June with light, airy puffs of delicate blossoms.

Hostas fill a woodland ravine with a blend of textures and shades along the path. They stand as stately clumps including *Hosta* 'Francis Williams' furnishing a background of wide, puckering blue-green leaves with an irregular yellow margin. The mosaic of texture and color possible today elevates hosta far beyond its beginning as a simple edging plant.

While large displays of color sweep through the beds around the garden, small, showy *Dianthus* sp. fit into the rock garden where their low-growing, fine texture set off the surrounding roughness of the stone. With them the small pink spheres of sea thrift (*Armeria maritima*) bloom in June, while a white carpet of April flowers cover the dark green, narrow leaves of candytuft (*Iberis sempervirens*). Here also one native perennial that blooms with a clear yellow composite flower of hairy, trailing stems grows from three to twelve inches and blooms from April to frost. This jewel of the rock garden, *Chrysogonum virginianum*, gives a showy effect for a long period. Gray plants like lamb's ear (*Stachys byzantina*) and the tiny, two-to-three-inch plant white sage (*Artemisia purshiana*) prefer the sandy, well-drained soil of the rock garden and soften the texture of the garden.

"To bring a garden to its peak," Emily emphasizes, "takes a lot of experimenting with color. And to find all the micropockets where there is good drainage or where there is more water takes time. So, many plants moved into the rock garden, where the soil is very porous, get four times larger than if they were sitting somewhere else under a tree."

By becoming familiar with the garden, continually experimenting, and keeping an eye on the design, Gilbert and Emily Daniels have achieved what most gardeners aspire to: a balance of ingenuity and simplicity throughout their landscape, from one gratifying season to the next.

- *Flowering deciduous shrubs form an attractive foundation for the garden throughout the year. Renewal pruning keeps these plants at their flowering peak.*
- *Put down composted wood chips in the summer to insulate roots from the baking heat as well as from the winter freezes.*
- *Pay attention to a plant's environmental needs. Sacrificing cultural requirements for design considerations will result in poor growth.*
- *Attractive ground covers become a colorful addition to the garden as well as textural backdrops. For many, one mowing a season serves to stimulate thick, compact growth.*
- *To enjoy the beauty of water lilies throughout the day, choose some cultivars that bloom in the early morning and some that bloom in the late afternoon.*
- *To avoid herbicide injury, follow the manufacturers directions explicitly.*

Oak Brook, Illinois

SUSAN BEARD

A suburban woodland cools the hot midwestern summers for Susan and Kenneth Beard of Oak Brook, Illinois. When they moved from the rolling Pennsylvania countryside over twenty years ago, they chose a home with comfortable tree-covered surroundings rather than the new open developments. Susan then began learning to adapt her Pennsylvania, Kentucky, and California background to the midwestern site.

Choosing a location already rich with trees and shrubs gave her a base from which to work, but the challenge came from the in-ground swimming pool the couple acquired with the house. Susan's techniques for successfully integrating the pool into the garden demonstrate many worth-while possibilities for midwestern gardeners.

The house opens onto a large terrace with the pool in the center. Two perennial borders flank the terrace, creating an intimate space for the pool as well as a sense of natural beauty for the pool area. The beds built around two twenty-foot rail fences change with the seasons, but the wood fences add texture and contrast well with the plants during the entire year. The contrast defines, and becomes counterpoint, in the garden. Although the fence directs traffic around the terrace and pool, it also visually ties the garden to the living space of the terrace.

The woodland spring comes with waves of yellow daffodils warming the view and

Sundrops (Oenothera tetragona) with the shrub cotoneaster.

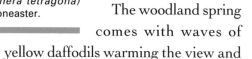

Left: Rising from a blanket of forget-me-nots (*Myosotis scorpioides*) are clumps of ostrich fern (*Matteuccia pensylvanica*); bulblet bladder fern (*Cystopteris bulbifera*); dame's rocket (*Hesperis matronalis*); *Hosta* 'Krossa Regal'; *Hosta sieboldiana* 'Frances Williams'; the fall-flowering aster 'Alma Potschke'; and lungwort *Pulmonaria saccharata*.

underpinning the rush of spring growth. By mid-April the subtle woodland native bloodroot (*Sanguinaria canadensis*) as well as the colorful Eurasian crocus have finished, leaving the stage to the endless flowering forms of narcissus. With a blanket of forget-me-nots (*Myosotis sylvatica*), these harbingers of spring reach back into the leafless woods, giving depth and brilliance to the landscape just emerging from six months of shades and shadows. The bunches of color withstand the late frosts and snows, bending without succumbing to the rapid shifts in temperature typical of the midwestern spring.

Unlike tulips and crocus, which can fall prey to squirrels, the narcissus and forget-me-nots represent some of the most carefree as well as welcome perennial spring-flowers. Susan recalls, "Squirrels came and picked every blossom and pulled out every bulb of an entire tulip collection one year, and there's not one coming up here now. They also eat crocus." Besides being tasty, tulips flower for only three to five years, after which the flowers become so small and crowded they quit blooming and must be dug and divided or discarded. Since the small bulbs flower again in two to three years, dividing rewards only the most patient gardener.

Stretching back into the trees, the narcissus flourish in patches of bright yellow. In the rich woodland soil, they bloom well without fertilizer. After a few years, as the single bulbs multiply, the individual flowers grow to bouquets. The bouquets become patches, and the patches grow together in sweeps of color, marking the end to a long midwestern winter with such dependability that they become a staple of the midwestern garden. Susan

Naturalized narcissus in early spring.

put enough space between the original bulbs to allow many years of bloom before they will require dividing to renew them.

The trout lily (*Erythronium* sp.), a native wildflower, comes up while the daffodils are still in bloom. The delicate little trumpets in white soften the intense sweeps of color produced by the daffodils and help move the woodland garden from the April fanfare to a strong background for the other seasons. By mid-May the peonies and irises mark the climax of spring.

Two large peonies bloom next to one fence near the terrace. With these Susan has a clump of orange poppies blending in color and contrasting in texture. Although the pink and orange poppies often bloom simultaneously, the colors mix with an electricity that warms the fresh spring days. The poppy's foliage dies back after blooming, though in the rich soil poppy seedlings spread throughout the area. Poppy seedlings will not bloom for several years, and they crowd together, preventing any from growing to flowering size. Most of the seedlings are pulled and discarded.

Experimenting becomes synonymous with gardening. Susan plans to try a new poppy, the mini cap, a cross between the oriental and the California annual poppy. She anticipates the new poppy will produce many more blooms per plant than *Papaver orientalis*, the standard perennial poppy for the area. Most poppies are planted when dormant in the fall. Although fertile midwestern soils grow vigorous poppies, planting in the late summer and autumn may not allow them to grow a deep enough root to survive. Also, most poppies resist moving. Establishing new cultivars re-

quires skill and luck. For this reason Susan plans to start with container-grown plants transplanted in the spring. Experimenting with growing conditions and marginally hardy plants provides information as well as interesting results. The wide range of conditions in the Midwest turns every garden into a test plot for some plants.

Reliable one-foot mounds of *Phlox divaricata* start blooming with the tulips, the creeping phlox (*Phlox subulata*) and the carpet of blue *Brunnera*, adding depth to the spring garden. Since *Phlox divaricata* roots deeper than creeping phlox, it tends to resist the dying out that is characteristic of creeping phlox. Also, a typical problem of creeping phlox is the invasion of grass into the mat of low growth at the garden's edge. The weeds become impossible to pull out without tearing up the shallow-rooted phlox, hence its reputation for delicacy. The sturdier *Phlox divaricata* grows from clumps, avoiding this problem, and the pale blue or white of the taller spring phlox blooms longer.

At the end of the swordlike stands of irises, huge, rounded leaves with crisscrossing veins gather for a quilt-like design. This *Ligularia* forms a lush backdrop. In another spot the smooth margins and wide, deeply veined leaves of *Hosta* 'Royal Standard'

Siberian iris 'Flight of Butterflies' and garden peony 'Do Tell'. in the background, Oriental poppy; American cranberry viburnum; and Theresa (the family pet).

Richland, Michigan
CAROLINE AND JACK GRAY

Caroline and Jack Gray garden in the shadow of history in the rich prairie soils near Richland, Michigan. Their home was built before the Civil War, and although it has undergone many changes, it retains the charm and grace of a bygone era.

"It's been an evolution of garden and house together. Our philosophy originally was that we wanted to live in our garden," recalls Caroline. As a matter of fact, Caroline and Jack so enjoyed the gardens of Dorcas Brigham, a professor of horticulture at Smith College, that they patterned their gardens, like hers, to surround them as part of their living environment instead of as a separate border on the edge of the property.

An easy transition between house and gar-

Little girl among the emerging Japanese painted fern (*Athyrium goeringianum* 'Pictum'); lady fern (*Athyrium filix-femina*); ostrich fern (*Matteuccia pensylvanica*); and columbine meadow rue (*Thalictrum aquilegifolium*) beneath a canopy of blackhaw viburnum (*Viburnum prunifolium*).

den creates a union between the two. Regarding their herb garden, Caroline comments, "The inspiration for this came from a marvelous herb garden that we visited in The Hague and Vita Sackville-West's garden in England. We're plant nuts who enjoy visiting gardens and seeing combinations and bringing these ideas to our garden. A lot of things, of course, have bit the dust. They simply can't tolerate this climate, but we've had a good time doing it."

The Grays' involvement with gardening extends back to their early married life when they moved to the Kalamazoo area from Massachusetts. Caroline explains that "one of the criteria for finding a place to live was good soil; that was

Left: Red poppy 'Mr. Lincoln'; foliage of the phlox yet to bloom; stars-of-Persia (*Allium christophii*); and pink peony 'Nick Shaylor'. In the background, irises; coralbells; campanula; rose garden; grape arbor.

really more important than the neighborhood. We wanted land that hadn't been stripped and wasn't subsoil in a subdivision. I think we were very young and innocent, and we bought this worked-out farm. So even though the village is Richland and this was a prairie with rich prairie soil, the husbandry hadn't been real red-hot here. They'd not enriched the soil, and we've had a lot of rebuilding to do."

Fortunately, the soil is a light, sandy loam unlike the heavier clay loam found in Caroline's nearby hometown of Lansing, Michigan. Thus the soil drains well. Caroline remembers, "My parents were always very envious because we could get into the garden at the end of March or the first of April, and they couldn't get in until the end of May."

To improve the soil over the years, Jack and Caroline have used compost as well as manure—the source of which involves one of Jack's other hobbies. He raises fantail pigeons, who can be heard softly cooing from the loft enclosure above the garage as you walk through the herb garden, and the pigeon litter goes into the compost. In the fall they put compost over all the beds to protect the plants over the winter and to replenish the soil with organic matter. Gradually the fertility and texture of the soil have been improved.

The design of the herb garden is both aesthetic and utilitarian. The herbs are confined to beds that are separated by the brick walk that surrounds them. As Jack reveals, "Years ago we had rows, but now they're in boxes" because they can easily become overgrown. Every spring he digs and divides the clumps to renew them, especially the fast-growing ones. Thus he controls their

Foliage of *Allium giganteum* with tulips; doronicum; peonies; and other spring flowers decorating the split rail fence.

growth, emphasizing with a sweep of his arm, "otherwise this would just be covered."

Texture plays an important role in the Grays' garden design. Caroline says that "like all gardens it has pretty spots and dull spots depending on the season. Things come and go." By choosing plants with attractive foliage and arranging them together to emphasize leaf texture, a perennial garden is beautiful, even when it is not in full flowering glory.

In addition to growing plants for the garden, Caroline enjoys flower arranging and uses as many plants as possible in this way. Pointing to a fall arrangement on the table, she notes, "All this came out of my garden. It's different on all sides—like my garden."

Indeed, Jack and Caroline have a great deal of variety and depth in the plants they grow. Always interested in seeing new plant combinations that work, they find that sometimes they are surprised by what Jack calls "happy circumstances of discovery and fulfillment."

Some of the plants Caroline uses for flower arranging are planted in rows behind the garden to assure her the quantities she needs, but many of these varieties are incorporated into the perennial borders as well. Also, very large plants like *Filipendula rubra*, *Miscanthus sinensis* 'Variegatus', and *Silphium perfoliatum* are easily five to eight feet tall and need to be placed at a distance from the house. Another such striking plant that Jack calls the "Midwest Gunnera" is the *Angelica*. Caroline explains, "When you go to Britain, they'll have these beautiful gardens, and they'll have plants with

Yellow tulips 'Jewel of Spring' bloom in front of *Doronicum caucasium*.

tremendous leaves—that's Gunnera." An easily cultivated substitute, *Angelica* grows eight feet tall, with two-foot round leaves with gracefully wavy margins and a treelike stalk topped with large white blossoms. Jack controls its growth at the edge of the garden by chopping it back and removing the flowers before it sets seed. He describes it as a powerful-looking plant that adds textural interest to an area kept in rows producing flowers for flower arrangements.

By contrast, near the house Jack and Caroline have a limestone retaining wall about two and a half feet tall that separates the formal rose garden and the reflecting pool and the more open, expansive portion of the yard. Along the top of the wall they have smaller perennials, more in scale with the garden near the house. In addition, the wall itself is home to a variety of small sedums and ferns that soften the stone and draw your eye to the detail growing there. Some of the plants in the wall include the grape fern (*Botrychium* sp.), ebony spleenwort (*Asplenium resiliens*), and a miniature hen-and-chickens (*Sempervivum ruthenium*). All of these and other miniature sedums give a very warm and interesting effect to the stone wall.

To extend a very attractive display, the Grays plant along the white rail fence that forms the north border of the formal portion of their garden: flowing expanses of sneeze-weed (*Helenium autumnale*) giving a golden show after the *Rudbeckia* 'Goldsturm' has finished blooming. Thus the white fence becomes a place for both consistency and change. The effect of the tall mounds of color against the fence extends from early July until frost, but the plants are different.

The temporal nature of perennial gardens offers a rhythm of its own. Caroline suggests, "Gardening brings many pleasures; it's fun to watch things come in. I'm not

A bed of *Helenium autumnale* and Cleome spinosa runs along a rail fence with grape arbor in the background. Photo by Pam Wolfe.

crazy about impatiens, but they are a patch of color all season." And as the trees grow, their increasing shade influences the evolution of the garden. Caroline recollects the garden as it was years ago: "We bought a pair of American bittersweet (*Celastrus scandens*) plants and put them along the farm fence, but it's too shady there now." Jack adds, "It wasn't always shady; things change, you know."

In addition to natural changes, Caroline and Jack enjoy experimenting with plants to find the best spot for them as well as to solve garden problems. One area under a group of trees needed a ground cover, so they moved lilyturf

(*Liriope*), which was outgrowing its spot in the flower border. After they moved it to the new location, they found it performed well. In fact, they enjoy the evergreen foliage and attractive flowers in the shadier area in addition to using it to hold down weeds like creeping charlie and nightshade. They combined lilyturf with hardy cyclamen, which is only six to eight inches tall and has long-lasting, dainty pink flowers during the fall. These two complement each other and fill a shady spot whose lack of light previously prevented all perennials other than spring bulbs from flowering.

Increasing shade can be an opportunity as well as a challenge. Jack describes a large walnut tree next to the house and garden as his biggest garden "nemesis." The problems caused by the lovely old tree are worse than those caused by the chipmunks and rabbits, who consider the garden their own burrowing ground and cause havoc eating bulbs and preventing the even drying of the soil around the roots of the plants they do not eat. The walnut tree releases a chemical that inhibits the growth of many plants. Twice Jack and Caroline attempted to cut it down, but it is so large and close to the house that the problems of removing it seemed a greater task than learning to live with it. Surprisingly, it does allow some plants to grow under its drip line while inhibiting others. A spectacular climbing hydrangea winds up the trunk, hanging gracefully out past the roof line of their house. The spring flowering display near this garden and vine is so beautiful, Jack and Caroline continue to struggle with the problems.

Although the grape vine on the arbor will not grow on the end near the tree, porcelian vine (*Ampelopsis*) grows very well. This lovely vine has yellow berries that turn blue, and it provides attractive foliage near the tree. Also, *Pachysandra* performs satisfactorily as a ground cover around its base. Other than the inhibition of certain plants, the tree is messy, dropping leaves and a sticky sap called honeydew, which causes a black sooty fungus to grow on the plants and walkways all summer.

Another problem that Caroline and Jack have to contend with is the Japanese beetle, which was not a problem in Michigan thirty years ago when they began gardening, even though the beetles had been very prevalent in Massachusetts. Heavy infestations of them are moving west, and the Grays learned the hard way how not to control them. Caroline recalls first having a few beetles on her roses, but not too many. However, in an effort to control them, she put out the traps that use the sex-attractant pheromone to attract the beetles.

"The first day we had half a bag full of beetles," she said, "and I thought that was terrible and then found a few of them on the dahlias. We thought one is good; we'll get a couple more. But none of our neighbors had them, so what we were doing was attracting every beetle in Kalamazoo County." A nearby fruit grower suggested that a mild infestation could be controlled by spraying plants with Sevin and very heavy infestations by spraying the lawn with Diazinon while they are pupating. Caroline and Jack do this in the fall after a particularly hard-hit season while the grubs are feeding on the roots of the grass.

Peonies are a standard feature in the midwestern garden, and they grow well in the sandy loam of this Michigan garden as well as in the heavier, more clay soils of other areas in the Midwest. They are affected by the same diseases as in other areas, and Jack follows the recommendation of removing dead foliage in the fall and disposing of it rather than composting it. This breaks the chain of infection from one generation to the next. As Jack notes, "Even then you get problems; botrytis is a mean problem. I spray them with the same stuff you would for black spot on roses. The main problem is the fella putting it on doesn't always do it often enough or when it is ideal. Those things never quit." Additional control of fungal diseases comes by pruning some of the large trees, which improves the light and air circulation in the garden.

In addition to using the typical rose fungicide on peonies for botrytis, other fungus-prone plants can benefit from such treatments. When the humidity is high and temperature swings keep the plant's foliage damp at night, monarda and phlox get powdery mildew, a fungus that discolors and destroys foliage. As a preventative, Jack begins spraying them when the temperature during the day reaches the nineties and the nights are also warm and humid.

Many single peonies grow in the garden now. Heavy double flowers often bend over and hit the ground. Even French hybrid tree peonies produce flowers under the leaves, making them difficult to see and giving the garden little satisfaction. Caroline remembers some beautiful doubles they had. "There was no way you could see them, and

Clematis grows along the Grays' picket fence.

so we finally got rid of them." Then, she points to two Japanese hybrid tree peonies near the arbor. "These are singles, and when they bloom they have two rows of petals and heavy yellow stamens. I'm really taken with single peonies, even herbaceous ones. They're up on top, and you don't have any problem with these tipping over."

From their living room window Caroline and Jack can view their early spring garden, as the forsythia and primroses announce the end of winter. The primroses flourish in the sandy loam, which drains well in winter but remains shady, cool, and moist in the summer. Quite often primros-

es have growing requirements that are specific and not always matched by midwestern conditions unless the gardener understands the growing requirements of the plants. Jack and Caroline start their primroses from seed and grow primarily *Primula* x *polyantha*, the more common dependable species. Although they do have some other colors, Caroline notes, "What I really like in the spring is yellow, and the orange and the white ones with the yellow eye—some combination of yellow."

Caroline encourages the primroses, a more delicate plant in the extremes of the climate, by knowing their cultural requirements and tending to them early in the spring. "Even before they start to grow, I'll begin. It takes me about three days along the path. I clean all the old foliage off them and feed them. This year I mulched them very heavily with shredded cedar shavings. I anticipated another devilish summer, so I thought I would give them a heavy mulch and they almost smiled at me. But look at the way they divided; they were happy with it."

Caroline loves to talk about her early spring gardening, "You're just dying to get at something. Early in the

A collection of hen-and-chickens *(Sempervivum tectorum)*; stonecrop *(Sedum)* with the orange stonecrop *(Sedum kamtschaticum)* in bloom; and little ebony spleenwort *(Asplenium resiliens)* growing in the wall; with the white *Dianthus deltoides*; coralbells; red pyrethrum above; and foliage of shasta daisy on the far end yet to bloom.

spring you've been cooped up in the house all winter long, and you can come out here and you're not where it's muddy because there's grass. You get down on your hands and knees and dig in the fresh dirt. It does wonders with your soul. That night you ache all over. You can't get comfortable in bed because all your muscles are screaming, but it's wonderful."

Another spring favorite is the Japanese roof iris (*Iris tectorum*), which is only about ten to twelve inches tall and has a flat beardless flower, resembling the Dutch iris. They are so well adapted that they spread in the garden by seeds, which sprout along the pathways. However, the growth is compact, the foliage is an attractive light emerald green, and generally the irises are a highlight of the garden during every season. By May, next to the walnut tree and the Japanese roof iris, the Virginia bluebells (*Mertensia virginica*), the lungwort (*Pulmonaria*), and the wood hyacinths (*Scilla hispanica*), which Caroline notes can become weedy, add shades of blue to the yellow of the early spring garden. During the summer and fall, the distinctive large, spotted leaves of *Pulmonaria* become the ground cover under the rhododendrons. Although most midwestern soil requires considerable acidifying to accommodate rhododendrons, the sandy loam of Michigan and northern Indiana can easily be amended to grow them.

Continuing around the house, one discovers another microclimate and another garden. A spectrum of day-lilies bloom in full sun during the midsummer, complemented by lavender *Monarda*. Their growing requirements and blooming times are similar, with slight differences in the texture and size of blooms, making them a good combination.

A reflecting pool and its fountain are the focus of another garden room.

Coralbells; pink painted daisies (*Pyrethrum*); stars-of-Persia (*Allium christophii*); phlox foliage; pink peony 'Nick Shaylor'; irises; campanula; rose garden; lupines; grape arbor; and climbing hydrangea.

Caroline explains that this water feature is the center of the rose beds. "The original idea was that we would make it a very shallow pool and have just sort of a blub, blub, blub fountain of sound and concentric circles. Then we got excited about water lilies!" She and Jack built the pool twice, and now the design is a five-by-three-foot rectangular pond two feet deep and made of six-inch-thick concrete. The overflow from the pool drains onto a

bed containing ferns that thrive with the occasional wash of water during a heavy rain.

Their water lily collection includes both hardy and tropical species that are handled like annuals and replaced each year. The hardy ones, however, are kept over winter in a bucket put into a pit in a spot protected from continual freezing and thawing. In addition to water lilies, Jack and Caroline grow papyrus (*Cyperus papyrus*), which they keep with the hardy lilies, and umbrella plant (*Cyperus alternifolius*), which easily survives in the greenhouse or sunny window. Next to the pool Caroline has planted crested irises (*Iris cristata*) for spring bloom and summer texture and gloriosa daisy for warm, glowing color in the hot summer sun.

"If you have open water like this, you almost have to put fish in it because of the mosquito population," says Caroline. Jack adds that during the winter, "We keep them in a big washtub in the basement" and notes that these contented fish breed and grow so well in the pool that he has to give some away each fall. The dimensions of water, sound, color, and life in their garden pool create an atmosphere of ease usually known only in milder climates.

When contemplating the struggles of growing a garden, Jack remarks, "You have disappointment all the time. There are so many different

plants, some surprise you and go up the scale and some go down."Although new gardeners will always want certainty, "there's no such thing for gardeners. It's a process that's very hard to get across. There are happy circumstances of discovery and fulfillment. For anybody who takes up gardening, discovery is awaiting them. It will be there if they keep going with it. They don't have to follow the book; in a sense, everybody has to go through this."

Left: Pink peony 'Nick Shaylor'; stars-of-persia *(Allium Christophii)*; and red poppy 'Mr. Lincoln' blend with coralbells; pink rose; campanula; and irises. In the wall are sedums; sempervivum; and ferns forming a rock garden. In the background, the grape arbor shades the porch and supports the orchids.

- *Even if you have rich, loamy soil, apply good conservation techniques; they will maintain that fertility. Ground that isn't amended with organic matter will decline.*
- *Create garden rooms that are living spaces with particular functions and styles.*
- *Remember that your trees will grow and extend the shade in your garden. Plan your garden to evolve appropriately.*
- *Some trees, walnuts being one of the most notorious, create an environment toxic to the roots of many plants. It will be difficult, but try to plan your garden around these challenges.*
- *Place sex-attractant traps well away from valuable plants. Luring problem pests to these traps may bring more of them to the garden than would have come originally.*
- *Mulch delicate plants like primroses as they begin to grow in the very early spring, to protect them against the late spring frosts and the drying summer days.*
- *Hardy water lilies need to be protected in an area, like a pit or window well, where they will not continually freeze and thaw.*
- *If you have a water lily pond use fish to help control the mosquito larvae.*
- *The texture of foliage is as important as the form and color of flowers. Considering the total impact of each plant will make your design more pleasing.*

and damp. This creative use of rocks and gravel yields more than aesthetic results in a rock garden. The special mixture creates an environment favorable to a wide range of plants. During years of little snow cover, the mulch insulates the underlying soil. During seasons of hard rain, the mixture and the garden's design help save the soil from erosion.

Also, top-dressing the beds with the sand, peat, and gravel mixture slows the growth of weeds. Likewise, removing spent flowers keeps them from self-sowing throughout the beds. Of course, weeding becomes a habit in any exemplary garden. The seven acres of meticulously maintained beds as well as the expansive prairie and nearby meadow are on a specific schedule. As a matter of routine, Marlyn rotates from one bed to the next. "Whenever I see a weed, I just pull it," she says cheerfully. "My pockets always have in them a weed or two. If you're going to have a flower garden, you must know what weeds look like. If you don't pull weeds when they are small, the flowers will be damaged by taking them out later. One of the first classes I took was one to learn to identify weed seedlings. This is particularly important if you're going to grow a lot of different plants from seeds. I take the seedpods off and sprinkle them where I want them." Keeping the beds weed-free gives the desirable plants room to grow.

Some seeds, like *Heuchera* 'Palace Purple', grow more dependably indoors in flats, and some shrubs Marlyn grows only from cuttings, like the Japanese maple. But all of Marlyn's plants grow with the sturdy splendor of plants fully acclimatized to their site. The lilies grow from the small bulbils at the base of the leaves. By taking these off and planting them in clumps of six, Marlyn assures that they naturalize through the garden according to a plan.

The self-seeding *Rudbeckia fulgida* comes in bright yellow drifts throughout the midsummer garden with only slight variation in form and size. These seeded plants are well adapted to the garden and may produce variations, as cross-breeding of the various dianthus cultivars do. With the dianthus, the original brilliant selections disappear with cross-breeding. Marlyn draws the line: "I have a big variety of dianthus, but I'm not going to replace those that cross and produce muddy-colored offspring."

Only the cactus garden contains little or no peat moss. Here many species of *Opuntia*, the prickly pear, grow easily. *Opuntia compressa* var. *microsperma*, as well as *O. microdasys*, *O. polyacantha*, *O. erinacea*, and *O. rhodantha*, survive the rigors of the climate when they are provided a rapidly drying soil. Another group of plants with the opuntias are the sedums, a variety of plants that grow vigorously

tucked between stones that connect them like mortar. The genus contains three hundred fifty species, many of which make excellent additions to the garden, along with the roughly thirty species of *Sempervivum*. Marlyn wishes other gardeners "wouldn't get their minds made up that things won't grow; I think if you want some you should try it. Two-thirds of the things I grow someone told me wouldn't make it."

The inorganic material will neither decompose nor harbor insects and slugs. For this reason the infestation common to many area gardens gives less cause for concern. A thick organic mulch can hide and feed organisms that will infest the garden. Avoiding bark chips, sawdust, and manure reduces many problems associated with the decay of organic material in the hot, humid season.

The lack of an organic layer may reduce microbe problems aggravated by high humidity. Also, the open site helps keep air circulating around the plants. As Marlyn notes, "I think that the plants stay healthier and have fewer insects if there's good circulation. Although I like to try everything, I don't grow things that give me problems. So many things do well. When the plants are healthy to begin with, they will stand up to the weather as well as to the pests."

This garden's pests are not just the small ones that need picking or spraying, but the four-legged variety roaming around in herds. Random pieces of fencing placed on its side throughout the garden discourage deer from wandering into the beds. Marlyn finds, "They'll jump a fence, but not when it's lying down like this."

Bright mat of *Dianthus deltoides*.

Marlyn says that healthy plants also depend on "a lot of fertilizing. I think it's important if you want a beautiful garden." The slow-release garden fertilizer works well when worked into the soil each spring, and adding a liquid fertilizer regularly promotes strong plants. Another technique Marlyn uses to encourage her plants and keep them from spreading

too freely is removing the flowers as soon as they are finished. This dead-heading keeps plants vigorous, stimulating vegetative growth and not allowing new seedlings to compete with the established plants. Plants like *Dianthus deltoides* spread quickly; dead-heading controls the garden's direction of growth and reduces future weeding.

The bulb garden begins with small scillas in March, narcissus in April, and tulips in May, followed by irises in late May and June. Then during late June and early July lilies crown the bed, starting with the simple, striking orange-yellow of meadow lily (*Lilium canadense*) and the exquisite yellow and deep orange bicolor of the rainbow lilies in June, to the wide variety of Asiatic and regal lilies that easily grow in the light soil. The loose, well-drained soil sustains the Asiatic, Chinese trumpet, and several species of lilies by providing them adequate drainage. Easter or Madonna lilies may reach five feet, topped with clusters of large white trumpets. One treasure among the collection, the stately martagon lily, has leaves gracefully emerging in a whorled fashion from a central stalk. Topped with masses of small Turk's cap flowers, the plant reliably provides a spectacular effect in the July garden.

The late-summer lilies are joined by the stately flowering onions, *Allium giganteum*, whose five-inch globes on

- *Start plants from seed, in the spot where they will grow, to select naturally those plants most likely to thrive in the rigorous climate.*
- *Mulching or top-dressing the garden with a mixture of sand, peat moss, and pea gravel improves drainage and reduces insect and disease infestation sometimes common with organic mulches.*
- *Space beds with the contour of the land so heavy rains will not wash away topsoil on hilly garden sites.*
- *To help identify the seedlings sprouting from a particular plant, place the seeds or bulbils in a grid of four by four. Recognizing this pattern as they grow identifies the plant.*
- *When the soil is amended with sand and gravel, many high desert cacti grow in the Midwest.*
- *Only a gardener's preference should determine which plants to attempt growing.*
- *A random maze of chicken wire lying through the garden discourages foraging deer and is inconspicuous among the foliage.*
- *Removing spent flowers or "dead-heading" keeps plants vigorous and slows the seeding of plants randomly through the garden.*

four-foot batons elegantly direct the summer show. As Marlyn notes, "From March to freeze I will have bulbs growing in this naturalized bulb garden." There are varieties collected from as far away as Denver by friends who know the special interest bulbs bring in Marlyn's garden. Among the bulbs, various cultivars of columbine (*Aquilegia*) fill out the spring display. During the early summer the compact Nippon daisy (*Chrysanthemum nipponicum*) backlights the flowers with clumps of white and yellow daisies beside and beneath the lilies. The outstanding succession of bulbs continues throughout the season in full view from Marlyn's living room window, bringing an elegant display indoors.

Each garden ties into a view from the house. From the bedroom a collection of silver leaves and white flowers glow in the moonlight. Compact, well-behaved artemisias like *Artemisia laxa* and *Artemisia frigida*, the fringed artemisia, reflect light from delicate gray leaves while the bright shadows from the flowers of *Aquilegia flabellata* var. *nana* stretch out like the talons of an eagle. Tucked among the dwarf conifers, the moonlight garden creates a unique sight all year. The cream-colored *Baptisia bracteata* has a slight yellow hue. Together with the weeping form of white pine and the unusual specimen of white forsythia, the moonlight garden thrives as a sep-

Pink painted daisy *(Chrysanthemum coccineum)*; white gas plant *(Dictamnus alba)*; perennial salvia *(Salvia x superba)*; oriental poppies *(Papaver orientale)*; perennial flax *(Linum perenne)*; and pink gas plant *(Dictamnus alba)*.

Threadleaf coreopsis *(Coreopsis verticillata)* with clumps of bright orange lilies (*Lilium* sp.) and yellow daylilies (*Hemerocallis* sp.).

arate—and romantic—room in the garden.

Moving away from the moonlight garden, color produces the theme as the gray tones are kept and shades of pink added to give the combination of pink and gray along a path near a line of white pines. The graceful pink buddleia sprouts each spring from the ground with its arching, flowering branches next to a new pink tamarax.

These fine-textured forms are brought out visually by the deep, soft red foliage and delicate single pink flowers of *Rosa rubrifolia*. The stately form of this shrub rose grows to seven feet and maintains its red rose hips into the winter. Nearby the pink boltonia adds a sturdy three-foot clump of small pink daisies in late summer and fall. These soft shades of pink behind the moonlight garden

accent the view from the house.

In addition to presenting a colorful display for every window's view, each combination has been arranged to go smashingly together. The pale lemon yellow flowers and gray foliage of the yarrow (*Achillea taygetea*) next to the soft pink *Dianthus allwoodi* 'Alpinus' blend well in a low sweep of color in June. The hot pink biennial 'Flashing Light' (*Dianthus deltoides*) spreads almost too easily in the light, sandy mix. The bright blue mounds of *Veronica latifolia* turn electric next to the cheerful patches of color. These displays are further set off along the three-tiered rock wall by surrounding sweeps of the fine-textured, lemon yellow of tickseed (*Coreopsis verticillata*), which also spreads easily among the stones. Along the path through the garden *Thermopsis montana* naturalizes into two-foot clumps of tall spikes of bright yellow flowers near the *Salvia* x *superba* 'East Friesland' and the *Achillea verticillata*.

Now the compositions may change as plants come and go through the hard years of little rain or those with hot, humid summers. As the salvia and flax flourish, the lamb's ears (*Stachys byzantina*) tend to melt out in the center and disappear. Native prairie plants easily withstand the wide swings, while the alpine plants take patience and care.

This Wisconsin garden reflects the loves of its dedicated caretaker. Surveying its extraordinary fullness, Marlyn calls her garden "pregnant." The metaphoric adjective is apt. At this plant lover's home, new life is always on its way to a beautiful and exciting place.

Hinsdale, Illinois

TRUDI TEMPLE

"You must see Trudi Temple's garden."

I heard these words again and again as I told midwestern gardeners that I was looking for gardens to feature in a book celebrating our region. So I got in my car and drove over to Hinsdale, Illinois, thereby taking a trip to a truly awesome garden.

Trudi Temple gardens one and a half acres about twenty-five miles west of Chicago. However, this garden could easily be distinguished as a world-class attraction anywhere. Her neatly brick-edged flower beds, slightly raised above the level of the lawn, absolutely burst with color. Trudi has organized her gardens to be in constant bloom and in such abundance that one mutual gardening friend of ours said of it,

White German statice, impatiens, Asiatic lilies, *Veronica*, and phlox light up the evening garden.

"After I've seen Trudi's garden, I just want to go home and burn mine."

In truth, she is an inspiration. Her energy and imagination redefine what can be done in this area of the country. Undeniably, her garden is a product of love and joy that she eagerly shares with those who are interested in learning how to turn the hot, humid Midwest into an oasis of bloom.

The first thing a new midwestern gardener will notice, other than the extremes of climate, is the predominance of heavy clay soils. Much of our topsoil earns the nickname "black gumbo"—"black" from the rich color of its highly organic content, and "gumbo" from the characteristic heavy stickiness its clay consistency lends when wet. Unfortunately, a homeowner in a

Left: Dropwort *(Filipendula purpurea)*; pink Phlox paniculata; maiden grass *(Miscanthus sinensis* 'Gracillimus')*; a nonseeding pink lythrum; and red monarda 'Violet Queen'.

new subdivision may find only a lighter brown clay, hardpan subsoil instead of the rich, dark topsoil. Many developers only top-dress the properties around new homes with an inch or so of topsoil instead of the six to ten inches common to much of our fertile heartland.

Showy flowering chives (*Allium schoenoprasum* 'Forescate'); foliage and buds of beardtongue (*Penstemon cobaea*); Oriental poppies; and buttercups (*Ranunculus repens* 'Pleniflorus').

The rich, dark topsoil and lighter brown subsoil both boast a wealth of mineral nutrients, but they both also pose a definite problem to gardeners. Even the topsoil has so much clay that it drains very slowly. During the growing season this alternate drown-

ing and suffocating test the tenacity of many garden plants. Finally, the rapid, repeated freezing and thawing during the fall and spring play havoc with plants' roots.

Why so much information about soil when introducing Trudi's garden? Because Trudi has gardened in the Midwest for twenty years, and she has solved the problem of our soils elegantly.

Trudi has made the soil in her garden lighter and its drainage faster by adding composted organic matter like leaves and grass clippings. What makes her composting method very exciting is where she composts. As she puts it, she "makes" her own soil by composting right in the ground. She finds a spot where she can still dig a little hole about eighteen inches deep, or she takes up a plant to make a new hole. Then she rakes everything right into it and fills it up about 90 percent with anything organic she has, avoiding meat products and plastics. After that she covers the last 10 percent with soil. Finally, she puts a flagstone on top to mark the spot and in places to serve as stepping stones through her garden. As soon as a stone sinks even with the ground level she plants directly into it. Trudi did not want a compost pile, yet she knew she had to do something about the soil. Having an enormous amount of debris, she decided that the best thing to do was to bury it. This is her own

unique system, and she eagerly teaches other would-be gardeners the benefits of soil modification. Amazingly, the proportion of soil to organic debris is such that the whole process takes only about six months. What wonderful gardens we will all have now that more and more sanitary dis-

Spirea 'Snow Mound'; white garden heliotrope; French tarragon; Siberian iris; lily 'New Poet's Dream'; bleeding heart; and alyssum (*Alyssum murale*).

tricts are prohibiting curb-side collection of leaves and grass clippings!

Another lesson gleaned from Trudi's garden is "never let a weed go

Right: Bright yellow creeping buttercup (*Ranunculus repens* 'Pleniflorus') with deep blue Hungarian speedwell (*Veronica latifolia* 'Crater Lake Blue').

Central Indiana

MARILYN MADDUX AND NELLIE OXLEY

Marilyn Maddux and Nellie Oxley are neighbors and gardening friends in Wingate, Indiana, who share plants and ideas. Despite their proximity, theirs are two distinctively different gardens. As Marilyn points out, "Everybody does things differently. You could go to a dozen gardens and none would be the same."

Marilyn describes her garden as an ongoing process. "It's evolving on its own, really. I can't say that I've got a plan. I'm like a gal I read about. I have a plant in my hand before I know where it's going to go." Although she develops a general plan, the details emerge while she's gardening. As a result of this extemporaneous technique, she often moves herbaceous perennials as well as bushes and trees. Marilyn smiles, remembering that her

It's July and a brilliant orange Asiatic lily blooms along Nellie's side

husband once told her she was the only person he knew who would rearrange trees. "I don't think I'll ever be done, and I don't want to be." Referring to a professionally landscaped garden, she admits, "If I got in there, I'd just have it all messed up. I'd want to rearrange something." Even though she hopes to achieve her master garden plan in three or four years, she acknowledges that her garden may never be finished.

When Marilyn begins a new area, she starts by choosing one of her favorite plants or colors. Shades of larkspur blend well with the light apricot hybrid tea rose 'Apricot Nectar'. The blue of the larkspur complements the apricot rose, as the pink and white larkspur fill out the arrangement. Simplifying

Left: *Rudbeckia fulgida* 'Gloriosa Daisy'; rose yarrow (*Achillea millefolium*); rose campion (*Lychnis coronaria*); and the foliage and dwindling flowers of columbine (*Aquilegia* sp.).

her method, she comments, "Once I start, I just keep going, putting in a few more to fill in. Every year things change a little bit. All the colors flow together. I don't think you can do anything wrong with flowers. It's all what you like." With a creamy white glow, 'French Lace', a floribunda rose, highlights plants in a group. Marilyn

Lamb's ear (*Stachys byzantina*).

believes that including white flowers "sharpens up everything."

Her garden evolves with memories as well as color. She enjoys the hybrid daylilies given to her by a friend. She points and says, "Those came from a neighbor of my daughter who lives in Illinois. The neat thing about garden-ing, whenever you go anyplace people give you something."

An added advantage of sharing plants is that when some plant dies out, it can be easily replaced with this midwestern generosity. Eventually everyone loses some treasured plant, and then having friends with a stand-in comes in handy. Says Marilyn, "I have given these irises to everybody in the county, and now I'm going to have to go back around and find the ones that I've lost. That's one thing good about sharing."

Marilyn and Nellie certainly practice this plant sharing, and when one has a new idea the other is certain to hear about it. Both women recognize, though, that their gardens really demonstrate that every garden is unique.

A gently curving walk winds through Nellie's backyard. She builds the beds along both the walk and the fence at the side of the property. The garden nearly fills her yard, surrounding her house and garage.

For annuals like dwarf snapdragons, moss rose, and sweet alyssum, as well as for early-spring perennials like *Phlox subulata*, creeping phlox, and *Verbena canadensis*, a low-growing, hardy verbena, Nellie uses the burned-out stump of a large tree as a planter beside the brick sidewalk. This enormous charred planter sets off the bright colors with the natural twists and turns of the buttressing roots. Like Marilyn, Nellie's garden reflects her own creative spirit, and with a sweeping gesture Nellie comments, "I made these beds symmetrical. You're not supposed to do that with flowers." But Marilyn quickly interjects, "You do them however you like."

One lovely perennial salvia, *Salvia* x *superba*, blooms for several weeks and spreads without becoming invasive. The combination of its gray foliage and deep purple spikes sets off many plants in June. Regarding perennial salvia, Marilyn notes matter-of-factly, "Nellie's given that to everybody—she's given it to me two or three times!" Even neighbors experience different success rates with the same plant.

One perennial verbena, *Verbena canadensis*, grows easily in the small areas near Nellie's house and walkway and blends well with rock cress (*Arabis caucasica*). The nearly chartreuse *Sedum acre* fills in the narrow space left between the house and the walkway. It spreads easily and readily forms a thick mat growing over the edges of the sidewalk, softening the geometric coldness that concrete walks can sometimes produce. These low-growing plants provide low-maintenance color all season. Although *Sedum acre* easily covers exposed sites, it invades lawn areas without some kind of edging. Sedums can also withstand the hot, often dry midwestern summers. The round, lavender spheres of the small, spring-

scilla. They are a vigorous ground cover for sites such as this and can highlight the shady slope. Also, in an effort to encourage more growth under the large maple, some pruning let in more light and improved air circulation.

Polly had to find a substitute for the fall show of chrysanthemums. Mums became too tall and leggy under the canopy of light shade, so the fall red aster 'Red Alert' adds a change. The heavy clay soil, combined with the late-spring and early-fall freezes, presents an additional disadvantage to mum culture. Mums are just about as sturdy as most roses here.

Mostly Polly trusts the region's favorites. "Anything that's native in a perennial garden is by far the best plant. Goldenrod, rudbeckia, columbine, and coreopsis are found in a native form in Wisconsin. These or hybrids of the native are the best plants for the perennial garden." 'Zagreb' and 'Moonshine' in addition to the native tickseed (*Coreopsis lanceolata*) are cultivars of coreopsis that grow vigorously and are among her favorites. Coralbells (*Heuchera sanguinea*) grows well in the well-drained areas of the rock garden, but the native species, *Heuchera americana* and cultivars like *Heuchera micrantha* 'Palace Purple' have lovely mahogany foliage with wispy mint-green flowers

A view of Polly's garden and the wide, circular path from her front porch.

and perform dependably like a true native.

Still, the fact that a plant is native does not ensure success. Attention must be paid to the type of habitat each plant needs. Looking at the plant in the wild gives the best clues for its culture. The wild lake iris found on calcareous, windswept cliffs needs a similar spot in a garden. A gift of an iris from northern Wisconsin, planted in the same type of rocks facing west but shaded by a tall maple, mimics the native spot.

Even so, gardening in the Midwest is unpredictable. Besides the dramatic swings in temperature, each year differs from the one before. Late freezes and early thaws control the hardiness of plants as well as the timing of flowering. Each season presents unexpected joys and disappointments. The cliche that midwesterners discuss the weather in polite conversation may seem quaint to gardeners in more steady climates, but ten inches of snow on a garden full of tulips, grape hyacinths, and doronicum naturally provoke conversation. Polly recalls, "You never know from one year to the next. Last year two groups of visitors came before May 16 and stayed about ten minutes because it was so windy and cold. Unfortunately, sometimes

Dalberg daisy *(Dyssodia tenuiloba)*; catmint *(Nepeta mussinii)*; and the multistemmed, small tree Juneberry *(Amelachier arborea)*.

Under a basswood in front of the house, Erwin's wildflower garden includes phlox, violets, ferns, sedges, trillium, and hepatica. Photo by Pam Wolfe.

For most gardens an invasion of violets often indicates wet soil, so weedy violets can become a major pest in a wet woodland garden, strangling all the competition with their thick rhizomes and heavy foliage. Pulling them out as soon as they appear controls the population and allows room for less aggressive violets like *Viola striata*, whose pale cream-colored flowers are gracefully borne on long stems from neat rosettes of leaves. Other desirable violets include *V. canadensis* and *V. corymbosa*.

With such a thick layer of small wildflowers Erwin says that "the major frustration is getting to the garden areas to weed without stepping on everything. I've thought of a major device like a boom. A large branch fell and is now a walk to get to the stuff I don't want to step on. If you walk on trillium early in the fall, you'll kill it. They're actually protruding a half-inch out of the ground, and as the year progresses they keep growing slowly. It's not so much weeding now but tearing out things that get too rambunctious. Most of the native things do really well once you can get enough mulch so you don't have a weed problem."

A nearby combination of ajuga and

sweet woodruff (*Galium odorata*) flower at the same time, and later their contrasting light and dark green foliage produces a Eurasian tapestry. The galium holds the aggressive ajuga in check while complementing it entirely. The dark bronze-green of the ajuga, with its short stalks of light blue flowers, is the backdrop for the finer-textured, pale green foliage of the sweet woodruff, which is blanketed in spring with tiny white flowers. The irregular sweep of yellow-green and white lightens the shady woodland garden.

Wildlife enters the garden as if it owned the place. Whitethroat sparrows come and outlast their normal stay to clean up on a large slug population encouraged by the humid weather. The parade of skunks, opossums, and raccoons, who get a free ride to the forest preserves, is almost overwhelming. Even deer find solace in the cover of the woodland refuge. With a small sweeping gesture, Erwin acknowledges, "If you didn't hear anything, you'd think you were in the middle of the woods because we're well screened. We have just the noise from the crush of people. A lot of people come to expect noise and wouldn't want the maintenance. After a certain time the maintenance gets easier. I'm gone for three and a half months a

Along one side of the path is a red azalea with pink, fringed bleeding heart; along the other Erwin also grows white false rue anemone.

Mixing this soil helps form a transition layer to which she adds a blanket of the composted manure and bark. The crowns of irises and daylilies rot easily and receive the very lightest topping.

Lynda meticulously cleans her beds each fall before any winterizing takes place. She emphasizes, "If I left a mess of dead foliage to clean up in the spring, I'd be behind before I could get started. Spring is my busiest time, and I can't add to it by waiting to clean out dead plant material."

During the dreariest winter days, the evergreens, once camouflaged by an array of blooms, stand as silent sentries adding form, color, and texture to the landscape. Before them, the fall color of the understory trees— tulpelo (*Nyssa sylvatica*), redbud (*Cercis canadensis*), and mountain maple (*Acer spicatum*)—create a head-turning display for weeks. In the Midwest, where the intense short summers develop to everyone's relief into glorious autumn days, seasonally spectacular trees and shrubs are an integral part of the garden.

Small trees or shrubs, like the Japanese tree lilac (*Syringa reticulata*), become part of the flowering display during mid-June when the herbaceous part of the garden is in full swing. The foliage, form, and even color and texture of the bark make the woody plants treasures of the garden. Not enough can be said for using a

good selection of trees and shrubs as bones and highlights in the landscape.

Garden sculpture has long found a place in the great estates of the world. Here in the Midwest, a fanciful fire-engine red enameled fox jumps out from plumes of red, white, and pink astilbe in Lynda's garden. This little fox grins capriciously from behind a

Juniperus horizontalis; rose yarrow (*Achillea millefolium* 'Red Beauty'); and, in the background, iris, Asiatic lilies, and perennial blue flax.

tree with such energy as to delight the viewer. Lynda places the sculpture in the bed and allows the plants to grow around it, partially hiding it during some of the year. The figure seems to change throughout the year along

with interesting changes in the garden.

Bulbs are planted deeper than recommended, and about two feet of oak leaves are blanketed on all the beds to protect them from the ups and downs of temperature. Regardless of soil preparation, Lynda finds, "You have to really winterize things. Although I don't have oak leaves, I pick them up off the street. I prefer them not mowed, because then they don't get goopy; they stay fluffy. I am at the point that I go out and mound the roses up with dirt to my armpits and then put on mountains of oak leaves! But I prefer to use composted manure. Then you don't have to worry about cleaning up in the spring, and besides, the leaves blow all over. Also I love the look of dark composted wood chips and manure around the beds in the summer." Shoveling giant piles of snow onto the beds from the walks adds one more layer of winter protection against those springlike, freakish days in January, which send all the wrong signals to the dormant plants.

Having been uncovered from their winter mulch and brought into the light of day during April, the roses bloom by June in all their glory. The rose garden next to the patio spills into a sunny patch of her neighbor's yard, spreading the pleasure they provide.

Chrysanthemums must be thoroughly winterized to survive. Even with the best care, some plants don't

survive the winter. Chrysanthemums, like many hybrid roses, suffer in the midwestern climate. Late freezes lift mums out of the ground. Rapid freezing in the fall, when the ground is still saturated and the plants are not yet fully dormant, kills roses. As the more demanding specimen roses die off, Lynda replaces them with sturdier floribundas like 'Betty Prior', the single pink flowering form that stands well in the heat and humidity. In addition, many specimen peonies and lilies fill out the bed as the delicate roses die off.

In order to locate the spring-flowering bulbs after the foliage dies and to identify the collection of daylilies, Lynda keeps a garden diary. An accurate record becomes a resource as well as an account of details. Initially, writing on stakes helps identify all cultivars, but the technique of actually cataloging plants can include more information. Often the stakes would come out of the ground and get lost. "This is my own project to try to keep track of everything and where I got it. It is fun to write down cultural information next to a photo. As each daylily comes into bloom, I go out and photograph it, recording it, because after awhile they begin to

Budding delphinium in front of rose yarrow (*Achillea millefolium* 'Red Beauty'); showy, pink evening primrose (*Oenothera speciosa*); yellow yarrow (*Achellia* 'Moonshine'); foliage of phlox, liatris, Asiatic lilies, and irises; and *Lythrum* 'Morden Gleam'.

- *To grow a thriving garden, deliver the right amount of water to a bed when it is needed.*

- *To help keep soil moist during dry periods, add an abundance of peat moss and composted manure when planting.*

- *Add one-third by volume of sand to a planting bed to improve drainage in heavy, clay soils.*

- *Grow plants in raised beds for access to the garden earlier in the spring.*

- *To winterize beds, blanket them with compost, peat, and sand.*

- *Bury roses with two feet of soil before layering on the mounds of composted wood chips and manure.*

- *To help follow and plan your garden, keep an accurate garden diary.*

Lynda fills an area with pink, showy evening primrose (*Oenothera speciosa*); light blue delphinium 'Belladonna'; rose yarrow (*Achillea millefolium* 'Red Beauty'); delicate yellow yarrow (*Achillea* 'Moonshine'); red Asiatic lilies; fading tulip foliage; foliage of liatris, aster, chrysanthemum, and phlox yet to bloom; and blue veronica. In the background, shasta daisy.

look alike." Lynda also puts labels in the garden because each week it looks different.

Lynda has a carefully considered, successful response to every challenge her garden presents. But her techniques tell only part of the story. Creative energy spurs her every gardening move, as she produces a flow of color from season to season, as she fills a hillside with continuous bloom.

- *Growing roses in the Upper Midwest requires digging up the plant each fall and burying it.*

- *Using All-American Selection (AAS) plants provides plants grown successfully over a wide range of environmental conditions.*

- *Plant aggressive perennials in ten-gallon buckets buried with the bottom cut out to prevent them from spreading out by rhizomes. This method also helps keep track of plants like poppies, whose foliage dies back after flowering.*

- *Cover your arms and legs when you cut off the seed heads of irritating plants like Dictamnus to prevent rashes common in many people.*

- *Seedpods and dried flowers from many perennials make attractive flower arrangements for the fall and winter.*

- *Tomato cages are an economical and efficient method of staking tall clumps of perennials.*

- *Starting perennials from seed takes two years. For the first year, keep seedlings in small pots or containers and mulch them very thoroughly during the first winter.*

Behind the iris foliage, a clump of white balloonflower (*Platycodon*); yellow yarrow (*Achillea*); tiger lilies (*Lilium tigrinum splendens*); spent shasta daisies; blue and white delphinium; garden phlox; cardinal flower (*Lobelia cardinalis*); and gloriosa daisy. Photo by Pam Wolfe.

Appendix

Gardens to Visit

Visiting gardens provides one of the very best ways to see a region, learn which plants grow best, and experience some beautifully arranged gardens. The following is a short list of Midwest gardens open to the public. Call ahead for times and fees.

In Illinois:

Anderson's Gardens, Inc., 2214 Stoneridge Dr., Rockford, IL 61107, 815-877-2525, reservations required.

Cantigny, 1 S. 151 Winfield Rd., Winfield, IL 60190, 708-668-5161.

Chicago Horticultural Society Botanic Garden, Lake-Cook Rd., Glencoe, IL 60022, 708-835-5440.

Morton Arboretum, Lisle, IL 60532, 708-719-2400.

In Indiana:

Foellinger-Freimann Botanical Conservatory, 1100 S. Calhoun St., Foster Park, and Lakeside Park, Fort Wayne, IN 46802, 219-427-1267.

Horticultural Society of the Indianapolis Museum of Art, 1200 West 38 St., Indianapolis, IN 46208, 317-923-1331.

In Iowa:

Dubuque Arboretum and Botanical Gardens, 3125 W. 32nd St., Dubuque, IA 52001, 319-556-2100.

Dr. F. McDowell, 1118 E. Court St., Iowa City, IA 52240, 319-338-2338.

Riverside Gardens, U.S. Route 151, Monticello, IA 52219, 319-465-3898.

In Michigan:

Fernwood Nature Center, 1338 Rangeline Rd., Niles, MI 49120, 616-695-6491.

Matthaei Botanical Gardens, Ann Arbor, MI 48105-9741, 313-998-7060.

In Minnesota:

Minnesota Landscape Arboretum, Chanhassen, MN 55317, 612-443-2460.

In Wisconsin:

Boerner Botanical Gardens of Milwaukee County, Whitnall Park, 5879 S. 92nd St., Milwaukee, WI 53201, 414-425-1131.

Olbrich Botanical Garden, 3330 Atwood Ave. Madison, WI 53714, 606-266-4731.

Mail-Order Sources

When the snow begins to fall, gardeners turn to catalogs. We all like to spin dreams and plans by paging through the offerings of various mail-order nurseries. These are some of my favorites, and the favorites of the gardeners featured in this book. I recommend them for pleasant January reading.

Anderson's Daylily Garden, 7909 Placing Rd., Indianapolis, IN 46226. Specializing in daylilies.

Bluebird Nursery, Inc., P.O. Box 460, 521 Linden St., Clarksan, NE 68629. Wide variety of perennials.

Bluestone Perennials Inc., 7211 Middle Ridge Rd., Madison, OH 44057. Inexpensive "six-packs."

Borbeleta Gardens, Inc. 15980 Canby Ave., Faribault, MN 55021. Daylilies and irises.

Busse Gardens, Route 2, Box 238, Cokato, MN 55321. Wide range of perennials.

Charles Klehm and Son Nursery, Route 5, Box 197, South Barrington, IL 60010. Extensive, established collections of peonies, daylilies, hosta, and companion plants.

Davidson-Wilson Greenhouses, Route 2, Box 168, Crawfordsville, IN 47933. Specializing in unusual geraniums (Peleragonium).

Dry Seas Prairie, P.O. Box 527, Warrenville, IL 60555. Local seed source.

Dutch Gardens, Inc., Dept. MN, P.O. Box 168, Montvale, NJ 07645. Inexpensive, quality bulbs.

Englerth Gardens, 2461 22nd St., Rt. 1, Hopkins, MI 49328. Iris, hostas, daylilies and companion plants.

Hauser's Superior View Farm, Route 1, Box 199, Bayfield, WI 54814. Quantity rates of northern field grown plants.

Henry Field's Heritage Gardens, 1 Meadow Ridge Rd., Shenandoah, IA 51601. Popular perennials packed in 2 1/4" pots.

Holbrook Farm and Nursery, Rt. 2, Box 223B, Fletcher, NC 28732. Quality perennial collection.

Homestead Farms, Rt. 2, Owensville, MO 65066. Daylilies and hosta.

Jackson & Perkins, 1 Rose Ln., Medford, OR 97501. Roses, bulbs, and companion plants.

Lafayette Home Nursery, Lafayette, IL 61449. Seeds of prairie grasses, forbs, shrubs, and trees, some non-natives also.

Lee Gardens, P.O. Box 5, Tremont, IL 61568. Variety of perennials, plants shipped bare-root in peat.

McClure & Zimmerman, 108 W. Winnebago, P.O. Box 368, Friesland, WI 53935. Wide range of bulbs.

Midwest Wildflowers, Box 664, Rockton, IL 61072. Seeds of native and nonnative wildflowers.

Milaeger's Gardens, 4838 Douglas Ave., Racine, WI 53402. Wide range of perennials.

Park Seed, Cokesbury Rd., Greenwood, SC 29647. Wide range of seeds, bulbs, and plants.

Pickering Nursery, Inc., 670 Kingston Rd., Pickering, Ontario, Canada L1V 1A6. Specializing in roses.

Prairie Nursery, P.O. Box 306, Westfield, WI 53964. Native wildflowers, grasses, plants and seeds.

Shady Oaks Nursery, 700 19th Ave. N.E., Waseca, MN 56093. Northern grown woody as well as herbaceous plants.

Soules Garden, 5809 Rahke Rd., Indianapolis, IN 46217. Specializing in daylilies and hosta.

Thompson & Morgan Inc., P.O. Box 1308, Jackson, NJ 08527. Wide range of seeds, bulbs, and plants.

W. Atlee Burpee & Co., 300 Park Ave., Warminster, PA 18991. Wide range of seeds, bulbs, and plants.

Wayside Gardens, 1 Garden Ln., Hodges, SC 29695. Wide range of woody and herbaceous plants.

White Flower Farm, Litchfield, CT 06759. Extensive perennial collection.

Van Engelen Inc., Stillbrook Farm, 313 Maple St., Litchfield, CT 06759. Quantity collections of a wide range of bulbs.

Plant Nurseries

For a gardener, a trip or two each year to a favorite nursery is like a trip to the candy store for a small child. Also, it's great fun to stop off at different nurseries when you travel around the Midwest. I cannot list all the nurseries in the region, but here are some of the ones I like to visit.

Ambergate Gardens, 8015 Krey Ave., Waconia, MN 55387, 612-443-2248.

Cottage Garden, Piasa, IL 62079 (20 minutes north of Alton), 618-729-4324.

Duane Carey, Iris Farm, Romney, IN 47981, 317-538-2575.

Englerth Gardens, 2461 22nd St., Rt. 1, Hopkins, MI 49328, 616-793-7196.

Gowen's Gardens, 6440 Hazeltine Blvd., Excelsior, MN 55331, 612-474-3536.

The Growing Place Nursery & Flower Farm, 25W471 Plank Rd., Naperville, IL 60540, 708-355-4000.

Midwest Groundcovers, IL (Route 25, north of St. Charles), 60174, 708-742-1790.

Milaeger's Gardens, 4838 Douglas Ave., Racine, WI 53402, 414-639-2371.

The Natural Garden, 38W443 Highway 64, St. Charles, IL 60175, 708-584-0150.

The Planter's Palette, 28 W. 571 Roosevelt Road, Winfield, IL 60190, 708-293-1040.

Possibility Place Nursery, Monee-Manhatten Rd. (near Route 57), Monee, IL 60449, 708-534-8853.

Savory's Gardens, Inc., 5300 Whiting Ave., Edina, MN 55439.

Plant Societies

For many a new gardener, once the hook is set, learning more requires reaching out to groups interested in fostering special areas of gardening. Publications, friendships, and the sharing of knowledge sharpen the skills of every gardener. To find local groups, watch for their sales and flower shows.

American Daffodil Society, Inc., 1686 Gray Fox Trails, Milford, OH 45150.

American Hemerocallis Society, 1454 Rebel Drive, Jackson, MS 39211 (Daylily Society).

American Horticultural Society, 7931 East Boulevard Dr., Alexandria, VA 22308.

American Hosta Society, 5300 Whiting Ave., Edina, MN 55439.

American Iris Society, 7414 E. 60th, Tulsa, OK 74145.

American Peony Society, 250 Interlachen Rd., Hopkins, MN 55343.

American Rose Society, P.O. Box 30000, Shreveport, LA 71130.

Chicagoland Daylily Society, 124 Jefferson, Batavia, IL 60510.

Garden Clubs of America, 598 Madison Ave., N.Y., NY 10022.

Men's Garden Clubs of America, 5560 Merle Hay Rd., P.O. Box 241, Johnston, IA 50131.

Midwest Daffodil Society, 1252 S. Fairview Ave., Blue Island, IL 60406.

Midwest Hosta Society, 5300 Whiting Ave., Edina, MN 55435.

Minnesota State Horticultural Society, 161 Alderman Hall, 1970 Folwell Ave., St. Paul, MN 55108.

National Council of State Garden Clubs, Inc., 4401 Magnolia Ave., St. Louis, MO 63110.

National Gardening Association, 180 Flynn Ave., Burlington, VT 05401.

National Xeriscape Council, Inc., P.O. Box 163172, Austin, TX 78716.

Northern Illinois Iris Society, 285 Stonegate Rd., Clarendon Hills, IL 60514.

Perennial Plant Association, 3383 Schirtzinger Rd., Columbus, OH 43026.

Agricultural Extension Services

Perhaps the best source of gardening information is also the most accessible and inexpensive (free). The Cooperative Extension Service has an arm of the state's university agriculture department in every county. Under the auspices of the U.S. Department of Agriculture, the cooperative extension agent provides an invaluable service to home gardeners as well as to the farming community. Most offices have a training program for volunteers called "Master Gardeners." I met outstanding Master Gardeners throughout the Midwest and would like every gardener to get to know their own program. You can find your own county agent by checking in the phone book or by contacting the state university. Listed here are the universtiy addresses for some of the Cooperative Extension Services in the country.

Illinois:
Agricultural Experiment Station
109 Mumford Hall
College of Agriculture
University of Illinois, Urbana IL 61801

Indiana:
Agricultural Experiment Station
Purdue University
West Lafayette, IN 47907

Iowa:
Agricultural & Home Economics
Experiment Station
Iowa State University
Ames, IA 50010

Kansas:
Agricultural Experiment Station
113 Waters Hall
Kansas State University
Manhattan, KS 66506

Michigan:
Agricultural Experiment Station
Michigan State University
East Lansing, MI 48823

Minnesota:
Agricultural Experiment Station
University of Minnesota
St. Paul Campus
St. Paul, MI 55101

Missouri:
Agricultural Experiment Station
University of Missouri
Columbia, MI 65201

Nebraska:
Agricultural Experiment Station
University of Nebraska
Lincoln, NE 68503

North Dakota:
Agricultural Experiment Station
North Dakota State University
State University Station
Fargo, ND 58102

Ohio:
Ohio Agricultural Reasearch and Development Center
Ohio State University
Columbus, OH 43210

South Dakota:
Agricultural Experiment Station
South Dakota State University
Brookings, SD 57006

Wisconsin:
Agricultural Experiment Station
University of Wisconsin
Madison, WI 53706

Selected References

A gardener's reference material becomes solace when everything is going wrong. The advice "Look it up to make sure" keeps every gardener on track, and a garden library seems to grow as fast as the garden itself. Here are some selections for reference and inspiration.

Armitage, Allen M. *Herbaceous Perennial Plants: A Treatise on Their Identification, Culture, and Garden Attributes.* Watkinsville, Georgia: Varsity Press, 1989.

Beales, Peter. *Classic Roses: An Illustrated Encyclopedia and Grower's Manual of Old Roses, Shrub Roses and Climbers.* New York: Holt, Rinehart and Winston, 1985.

Bloom, Alan. *Perennials For Your Garden.* Chicago: Floraprint U.S.A., 1981.

Clark, Rose C. *Keys To The Trees Of The Chicago Region: Native and Cultivated.* Lisle, Illinois: The Morton Arboretum, 1988.

Clausen, Ruth Rogers, and Nicolas H. Ekstrom. *Perennials for American Gardens.* New York: Ekstrom, Random House, 1989.

Cox, Jeff and Marilyn. *The Perennial Garden: Color Harmonies Through the Seasons.* Emmons, PA: Rodale Press, 1985.

Decker, Henry F., and Jane M. *Lawn Care: A Handbook for Professionals.* New Jersey: Prentice Hall, 1988.

Dirr, Michael A. *Manual of Woody Landscape Plants.* Champaign, IL: Stipes, 3rd ed., 1983.

Embertson, Jane. *Pods: Wildflowers and Weeds in Their Final Beauty.* New York: Charles Scribner's Sons, 1979.

Giles, F.A., Rebecca McIntosh Keith, and Donald C. Saupe. *Herbaceous Perennials.* Reston, VA: Reston, 1980.

Harper, Pamela, and Frederick McGourty. *Perennials: How to Select, Grow and Enjoy.* Tuscon, AZ: HPBooks, Inc., 1985.

Heriteau, Jacqueline, with Dr. H. Marc Cathey. *The National Arboretum Book of Outstanding Garden Plants.* New York: Stonesong Press, Simon and Schuster, 1990.

Highshoe, Gary L. *Native Trees for Urban and Rural America.* New York: Van Norstrand Reinhold, 1987.

Keith, Rebecca McIntosh, and F.A. Giles. *Dwarf Shrubs for the Midwest.* University of Illinois at Urbana-Champaign College of Agriculture, Special Publication 60, 1980.

Lacy, Allen, ed. *The American Gardener: A Sampler.* New York: Farrar Straus Giroux, 1988.

Loewer, Peter. *American Gardens—A Tour of the Nation's Finest Private Gardens.* New York: Simon and Schuster, 1988.

Oehm, Wolfgang, James van Sweden, with Susan Rademacher Frey. *Bold Romantic Gardens.* Reston, VA: Acropolis Books, Ltd., 1990.

Ottesen, Carole. *Ornamental Grasses, the Amber Waves.* New York: McGraw Publishing Company, 1989.

Schulenberg, Ray. *Native Shrubs of the Chicago Region—A Brief Evaluation.* Lisle, IL: Morton Arboretum, 1975.

Snyder, Leon C. *Gardening in the Upper Midwest.* Minneapolis: University of Minnesota, 2nd ed., 1985.

Still, Steven M. *Manual of Herbaceous Ornamental Plants.* Champaign, IL: Stipes, 3rd ed., 1988.

Swain, Roger B. *The Practical Gardener: A Guide to Breaking New Ground.* Boston: Little, Brown, 1989.

Swink, Floyd, and Gerould Wilhelm. *Plants of the Chicago Region.* Lisle, IL: The Morton Arboretum, 1979.

Taylor, Norman. *Taylor's Encyclopedia of Gardening.* Boston: Mifflin, 1986.

Thorpe, Patricia. *The American Weekend Garden.* New York: Random House, 1988.

Time-Life Books. *The Time-Life Encyclopedia of Gardening.* Henry Holt, 1986.

Verey, Rosemary, and Ellen Samuels. *The American Woman's Garden.* Boston: Little, Brown, 1984.

Voigt, T.B., Betty R. Hamilton, and F.A. Giles. *Groundcovers for the Midwest.* University of Illinois at Urbana-Champaign College of Agriculture, Special Publication 65, 1983.

White, Katherine S. *Onward and Upward in the Garden.* New York: Farrar Straus Giroux, 1979.

Wyman, Donald. *Wyman's Gardening Encyclopedia.* New York: Macmillan, 1971.

Index

"I have grown wise, after many years of gardening, and no longer order recklessly from wildly alluring descriptions which make every annual sound easy to grow and as brilliant as a film star. I now know gardening is not like that."

—*Vita Sackville-West*

This is a list of plants discussed in this book that are commonly grown in Midwest gardens: standard choices, enduring favorites, and traditional beauties. After each plant are page numbers to turn to for advice. The gardeners discuss how that plant can be combined with others and what special conditions, if any, it requires. Since the lovely and wide-spread lilies need well-drained soils, they are most popular in areas with lighter, sandier soils. Peonies, on the other hand, flourish in the heavy clay and grow poorly when the soils are too sandy. Many garden standards suffer in hot weather with high humidity only to bounce back the next spring. By following the directions of these seasoned gardeners, even well-loved roses become a reliable midwestern selection.

A bold page number refers to a photograph.

Hosta (plantain lily), **12**, **13**, **82**, **88**, 167, 186, **187**
    helonioides, 16
    lancifolia, 16
    plantaginea, 16, 91
    sieboldiana, **19**, **30**
Hydrangea
    anomala petiolaris (climbing hydrangea), **29**, 33, 102, **105**
    arborescens, 83, **86**
    quercifolia (oakleaf hydrangea), 5, 83
Iberis sempervirens (candytuft), 41, 87, 140
Impatiens, **20**, 25, **26**
Ipomoea (morning glory), **158**
Iris, 22, **65**, 93, 94, 95, 96, **160**, 167, **175**, **184**
    cristata, 105
    Japanese, 42
    pseudacorus, 93, 143
    Siberian, **23**, **94**, **120**
    tectorum, 105
Kerria japonica, 33
Larkspur, 127, 129, 175, **177**. *See also Delphinium*
Liatris (gayfeather), 24
Lilium (lily), 26, 68, **116**, **138**, **165**, **166**, **167**, 194
    canadense, 114
Lunaria annua (money plant), 194
Lychnis (campion, catchfly)
    chalcedonica, 185, **194**
    coronaria, **129**, 157
    viscaria, 61
Lycoris squamigera (magic lily), 93
Lythrum (purple loosestrife), 23, 32, 84, **86**, **167**, 176
Magnolia, 82
Malva (mallow)
    alcea, 33, 139
    sylvestris, 23, **25**
Matteuccia pensylvanica (ostrich fern), **99**
Mertensia virginica (Virginia bluebells), 59, 105, 146, 148
Miscanthus, 64, 84, 100, **118**
Monarda (bergamot, beebalm), 23, 86, 105, **118**, 176
    didyma, 59
    fistulosa, 52
Myosotis (forget-me-not), **94**
    scorpioides, **88**
    sylvatica, **29**, 30, 90

Narcissus (daffodil), 67, 90, 175, 181
Nasturtium, 196
Nepeta (catmint)
    cataria, 5
    mussinii, 31, **31**, 33, 125, 139
Nicotiana (flowering tobacco), 176
Oak, 4
    burr, 47
    chinquapin, 47
Oenothera (evening primrose, sundrops)
    fruticosa, 24, 86, **89**
    missouriensis, **78**, 139
    tetragona, **34**
Pachysandra (spurge), 35, 102
    procumbens (alleghany spurge), 83
Paeonia (Peony), 103, **106**, 131, **182**, **183**, 185, **186**
Papaver orientalis (oriental poppy), 67, 91, **99**
Parthenocisus quinquefolia (Virginia creeper), 10, 56
Phlox, 59, 67, 103, 151, 192
    carolina, 78, **81**, 86
    divaricata, 91, 155
    paniculata, **2**
    pilosa, 3, **148**
    prairie, 46
    subulata, 23, 91, 130, **131**, 143, 173
Platycodon (balloon flower), **193**
Portulaca (rose moss), 160
Potentilla fruticosa, 5
Ranunculus (buttercup), 59, **121**
Rhus (sumac), 47
    typhina, (staghorn), 56
Ribes alpinum (alpine currant), 4
Rosa (Rose), 4, 6, 8, 25, 129
    bourbon, **32**, 33
    x *centifolia*, **31**,
    climbing, 30
    damask, 33
    floribunda, 68, 76, 77
    gallica, 33
    gallica officinalis, 30
    hybrid tea, 10, **105**, 129
    miniature, **195**
    polyantha, 10
    rubrifolia, 116, 162, 163
    rugosa, 33, 68
    setigera (prairie rose), **45**, 47
Rudbeckia (coneflower)

    fulgida, 9, **10**, 68, **96**, 102, 113, **128**, 140
    hirta, 7
Salvia
    pratensis, 24
    x *superba*, 115, 130
Scilla (squill)
    hispanica, 105
    siberica, 140
Sedum (stonecrop), 23, **104**, 163
    acre, 130
    spectabile, 173
Sempervivum (hen and chickens), **104**, **109**, 113, 163
    ruthenium, 101
Silene (campion, catchfly)
    regia, **48**
    vulgaris, 24
Spirea
    x *bumalda*, 9, 83, **120**
Stachys (lamb's ear)
    byzantina, 87, 117, **130**, 177
    grandiflora, 23
Syringa (lilac)
    meyeri, 33
    x *persica*, 83
    reticulata, 164
Thuja occidentalis, 55, **56**
Tulip, 101
Verbena canadensis (rose verbena), 130, **131**
Veronica, 41, 74, **138**, **143**, **159**
    alpina, **137**
    latifolia, 117, **121**
    repens, 160
    spicata, **78**
Viburnum, 4
    x *burkwoodii*, 83
    plicatum, 178
    prunifolium, 5
Viola, 41
    canadensis, **150**, 151
    cornuta, 59
    corymbosa, 151
    striata, 151
    tricolor (johnny jump ups), 30, **156**, **157**
Walnut, 102
Weigela florida, **69**
Wisteria macrostachya (Kentucky wisteria) 10, 64, **66**, **191**
Yucca filamentosa, **8**

Just as a musician's repertoire expands over the years, a gardener accumulates a wide range of plants and develops an assortment of gardening styles. Sometimes the garden gets larger, sometimes the theme just changes. Rock gardens, prairie gardens, rose gardens, English gardens, European fountain gardens, Japanese gardens, woodland gardens, gray gardens, herb gardens, butterfly gardens, and even exotic vegetable gardens take shape in the Midwest. In the hands of a skilled gardener, in a spot that is just right, rare and little used plants are as dependable as any. The following list highlights some of the less common, and more challenging choices used and discussed by the gardeners in this book.

A bold page number refers to a photograph.

About the Author

Pamela Wolfe's introduction to gardening took place in Crawfordsville, Indiana, where she was born and raised. She went on to receive a B.A. in botany from Ohio Wesleyan University and a masters in botany at Indiana University. She has served on several midwestern horticultural committees, including the University of Illinois Cooperative Extension Advisory Committee, the advisory committee for the Metropolitan Chicago Core Curriculum Project, and the college liaison committee of the Illinois Landscape Contractors Association. For three years, she was the president of the Metropolitan Agriculture Teachers Association. She also was one of the first women to teach agriculture in the Illinois public school system.

Ms. Wolfe still lives and works in Illinois. She developed vocational ornamental horticulture and teaches science at Willowbrook High School and is a part-time instructor at the Morton Arboretum, where she teaches horticulture, perennial gardening, and turf and ground cover management, and at North Central College, where she teaches landscape design. She shares her own Midwest garden in Downers Grove with her husband and two daughters.

About the Photographer

Gary Irving's specialty in color landscape photography is the hallmark of his four previous books, *Vermont*, *Chicago*, *Illinois*, and *Beneath An Open Sky*. His work has appeared in numerous publications, including *American Photo*, *Garden Design*, *Horticulture*, and *Chicago* magazine.

Mr. Irving has received the Studio Magazine International Award and the Creative Print Advertising and Design Gold Award. He lives with his wife and two daughters in Wheaton, Illinois.